Capitalism, Sustainability and the Big Society

Meeting the global challenge of ensuring a sustainable future.

David Rhodes

authorHOUSE®

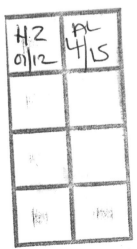

AuthorHouse™ UK Ltd.
500 Avebury Boulevard
Central Milton Keynes, MK9 2BE
www.authorhouse.co.uk
Phone: 08001974150

First published by AuthorHouse   04/01/2011

ISBN: 978-1-4567-7580-3

Cover photograph: The Old Market Square in Nottingham where Robin Hood may well have
pioneered an early version of the Big Society.
Certain stock imagery © Thinkstock.

This book is printed on acid-free paper.

Because of the dynamic nature of the Internet, any web addresses or links contained in this book
may have changed since publication and may no longer be valid. The views expressed in this work
are solely those of the author and do not necessarily reflect the views of the publisher, and the
publisher hereby disclaims any responsibility for them.

Preface

This book was originally conceived as a successor to *Manage IT*, which I wrote with Mike Wright in 1985. That became a recommended text for students at the Open University and has been published in several editions. But as I began to assemble my ideas and background cases it became apparent that while *Manage IT* is notionally about the effective and efficient use of information technology, it actually begins to address a more fundamental and perplexing issue which is the effect of technology on people's lives and fundamentally the way our society evolves. I had also become a director of Encraft Limited, a company which specializes in low-energy and sustainable solutions and was thus re-engaging with engineering projects.

This fortuitous combination of circumstances, opportunities and experience was particularly pertinent since among the major problems facing the world at present are sustainability, climate change, the fragility and injustices of the capitalist system, and extreme poverty. Indeed the financial crisis of September 2008 arose as I began writing the book which is now far removed from IT and inspired by my engineering experiences and the philosophical insights of Popper and Kant. The underlying theme is the evolution of human organization. The hypothesis is that a systemic change to capitalism is essential and leads inevitably to what Prime Minister David Cameron has called the *Big Society*. It explains why systemic change is necessary and what form it should take.

Much has been written about the nature of evolution some of it summarized here, but understandably it is mostly humankind's view of other forms of life. When we consider the human race it is usually our origins and relationship to apes which exercise us. We tend to see ourselves as special on a planet provided primarily for our benefit and rarely stop to consider ourselves as simply another species among many. We can dig up and identify species going back over millions of years and with reasonable certainty show which have progressed and which have become extinct, but we know little about the future. For the first time since we emerged as a species more than 30,000 years ago we have to worry about our effect on the environment as well as the effect of the environment on us! We do not know whether our evolutionary line is set to continue for eons or whether it will shortly peter out to extinction. Certainly we know the environment is changing but, adaptable as we humans are, can we adapt to such change and if so what form should the adaption take and how can we bring it about? And is climate change the only challenge?

This book is thus one person's perspective, unashamedly an engineer's point of view, but a serious attempt to examine humankind's ability to adapt. It is not the result of exhaustive research into the human condition – a potentially futile task for reasons of bounded rationality (see Chapter 2) - but it does set out to broaden debate. It dares to suggest that politics cannot solve the global problems referred to above without a modification to capitalism. In a nutshell, the world is too complex for managed, top-down solutions even if its leaders could agree on such things. What it argues is that we need systemic ideas which will empower the Planet's billions to take the world in the direction of a sustainable future and their own survival; a world which might also deliver a more equitable distribution of wealth. Somehow the capitalist system, which merely values those things which can be priced, must be made to also include those things which are of value to all humankind and the Planet as a whole; in short, the *Big Society*.

So, while *Managing IT* was simply about the exploitation of information technology, this book addresses systemic change.

The structure of the book is innovative; one might say half in the style of science and half in that of the humanities. There is a good reason for this. Evolution is determined by both, yet in the UK so many high-level decisions are made by people familiar only with the latter. We are in effect governed by half-ignorant people. This is a modest attempt to rectify the imbalance.

A second innovation is to present the line of argument chapter by chapter with references and illustrative examples posted separately as footnotes to each. In this way the relative purity of argument is not disrupted by the examples and the fact that examples are not always perfect illustrations of a point does not therefore confuse the text nor disqualify them (reality is simply not that tidy-minded). References in Chapter 1 are extensive and mostly provide evidence in regard to climate change and unsustainable activities. More generally the references are largely to classic works and few enough in number to encourage readers to turn to them for greater depth and breadth.

Overall, the book should confront readers, especially students, with ambiguities and alternative points of view. It will warn or remind them that in matters of people the answers are rarely found "at the back of the book". Yet "the second law of thermodynamics is totally unforgiving" and "truly bears on their lives".

I am indebted to the many organizations and individuals who have contributed help with projects, case studies, information, experiences and insights which have stimulated the thinking behind the book. Special thanks to my son Matthew, with whom I have had many useful discussions and who could have written a better version of this book had he had the time. Fortunately he has been otherwise occupied in developing Encraft Limited. I also offer my sincere thanks to my wife Jan, also an engineer, for carrying out the exacting task of checking various drafts of the text.

Eur Ing Dr David Rhodes CEng FIET FCIBSE

January 2011

Contents

Chapter 1:
Introduction

"Who sees with equal eye, as God of all,
A hero perish, or a sparrow fall,
Atoms or systems into ruin hurled,
And now a bubble burst, and now a world."

Alexander Pope (1688-1744)

The major challenges confronting humankind. Capitalism and the global crisis of 2008. Global poverty coexisting with extreme affluence.

Magic

My non-stop flights to Johannesburg made the point most forcibly. A gentle take-off from Heathrow in the early evening preceded by champagne and cocktails. Then, a choice of near-gourmet food, five courses with selected wines from every continent, coffee and a digestif. Depending on my mood, I could watch television, make a telephone call, use my computer, read, sleep, watch the latest film, drink more alcohol or catch up with the latest news. If I were lucky, some stranger would enliven the journey with conversation; a shoemaker, book publisher and a mercenary are especially memorable in this regard. Outside the air was too thin to support human life. Inside, a continuously updated display indicated air speed, distance to destination, our height and position on a map of the world. When I paid attention, I would typically discover that I was more than 12 km above the ground and travelling at around 1000 km per hour with an outside temperature of minus 50°C and an inner one of 21°C. Breakfast was served an hour before Johannesburg where I later disembarked with 300 others, unharmed, unruffled, refreshed and ready for work.

1

This was not all. The aircraft was soon on its way back to Heathrow. It had been technically checked and totally replenished as a living space. It would return again tomorrow and the day after that. It might occasionally change route but would continue to repeat the above trick of staying in the air unaided, for up to 12 hours at a time, for decades. It was, is and continues to be, magic [1.1, 1.2].

But sadly the magic is not powerful enough. Most of my flight was over Africa, stricken with poverty famine, a shortage of water, disease and conflict. How can such magic exist and yet remain impotent to help those just 12 km below where there are some of the most appalling examples of the human condition it is possible to find [1.3, 1.4] ? If I had simply jumped from the plane I would arrive in less time than it takes to boil an egg. The average annual income in Zimbabwe is barely enough to buy a meal for four in one of Nottingham's medium-priced restaurants and almost the whole of Africa below the Sahara suffers from a lack of clean water and inadequate sanitation. This is less due to a fundamental shortage than economic incompetence [1.5, 1.6, 1.7].

Ironically, every flight emits a large quantity of carbon dioxide [1.8]. UK airlines as a whole emit around 2% of all UK carbon dioxide (CO_2) which is very high for a minority activity and set to rise due to increases in travel by air. As emissions are reduced in other areas the proportion will thus rise, an issue which bears heavily on climate change despite improvements in aero-engine technology [1.9] and legislation [1.10].

Climate change

What are we to do about the changing climate? It is changing as the measurements of a rise in European summer temperature over the past 150 years illustrate [1.11, 1.12, 1.13, 1.14]. Whether this is due to human activity or a natural cyclic change the planet has experienced many times before, or even a combination of the two, maybe open to debate. It is of course misleading and statistical nonsense to take just one abnormal event as an indication of a trend since variations from such events extend either side of the moving average. The true average and trend become evident only after a period of time. However, the almost simultaneous and catastrophic heat wave in Moscow, the mud slides in China and the flooding in Pakistan (due to an exceptionally severe monsoon) during July and August of 2010, and the thousands of deaths which accompanied them, might be due to some movement in the path of the jet stream. If we truly understood the mechanism and it were linked to temperature rise, we could replace our dependency on statistical evidence with objective explanations. But this is not yet possible.

Satellite views of the Baltic in 2010 reveal an outburst of blue-green algae about 377,000 km² in area which, according to the World Wildlife Fund (WWF), is due in part to over-fertilization of the land. The chemicals are washed into the sea to cause dead zones which, with high air temperatures of up to 38°C and little wind or waves, thence encourage the evil-smelling weed. This weed can cause skin rashes and allergic reactions sufficiently serious for German coastguards to warn people not to swim in the contaminated water. Similar outbursts occurred in 2001 and 2005.

An unprecedented fall in the water levels of the Tigris and Euphrates rivers in Southern Iraq has caused a plague of snakes which, along with drought and heat are driving people from their homes. These two great rivers have supported life in the area for several thousand years but dams in Turkey and the diversion of water for irrigation have reduced the flow in the Euphrates from 950 m³/s in 2000 to 250 m³/s in 2009.

The most recent data from the US National Oceanic and Atmospheric Office confirms the trend for the Planet to become warmer. Measurements from around the world by independent scientists are consistent across ten key indicators, three measuring the reductions in glaciers, polar snow and ice and the other seven concerned with a range of land, sea and atmospheric temperatures. Each of the last three decades has been much warmer than the decade before. At the time, the 1980s was the hottest decade on record. In the 1990s, every year was warmer than the average of the previous decade. The 2000s were warmer still [1.15].

It is also important to note that computer simulations are seen to reproduce results which follow the historical records quite snugly. It might thus be rational to conclude that the simulation model is very close to simulating the real thing and that temperatures in the UK will continue to rise as those same computer simulations predict. The exceptional summer which killed so many in France in 2003 will thence be merely average by 2050 [1.16]. And, since simulation includes the effects of human activity and such activity, when separated from known variations in the sun and volcano cycles, explains the increase, it might also be sensible as a scientifically valid hypothesis (i.e. one which is testable and accepted unless shown to be false) to assume the cause is largely due to us [1.17]. In any event, whether due to our own actions or some planetary aberration, we need to take into account the rise in global average temperature, the accelerating melting of polar ice, release of methane and concomitant rises in sea level. Inhabitants of the UK in particular should note another plausible hypothesis, that an effect of climate will be to stop the Gulf Stream (Atlantic Conveyor). If this happens the UK could become very cold in winter [1.18].

The melting of polar ice is generally accepted as a good indication of global warming. There are huge quantities of ice and because ice has a large latent heat for melting the amount of heat needed to modify a polar ice cap is larger than an initial thought might infer. The heat required to merely melt a given quantity of ice would, if applied to a similar quantity of melted water at just above freezing point, raise it to 80°C. This is very hot and close to water's boiling point of 100°C. Therefore, if the volume of ice is diminishing you can be sure a very large quantity of heat has been absorbed.

Evidence that the area of ice is falling steadily and equally importantly also thinning, is incontrovertible [1.19, 1.20, 1.21]. In addition, the warming of Arctic ice and increasing sea temperatures are causing the permafrost to melt. The icy covering, which hitherto has held methane trapped below, then releases the gas [1.22]. Methane is 20 times more powerful as a greenhouse gas than carbon dioxide and the amount stored beneath the Arctic is calculated to be greater than the total amount of carbon locked up in global coal reserves. Greenhouse gases increase heat ingress from the sun, reduce the polar ice and consequently the heat reflected away. The Planet is getting warmer and in doing so is triggering effects which accelerate that warming. A recent study by Professor Corinne le Quere suggests that projected temperature rises will be higher than the 4°C previously postulated at around 6°C by 2100 [1.23].

It will be difficult, even impossible, for many people to adapt to conditions the human race has not encountered in more than 10,000 years [1.24]. Cutting our emissions is essential if the rise in average temperature is to be constrained to 2°C [1.25]. Nonetheless, our emissions continue to increase because any reduction by the developed nations is offset by an increase in the developing world [1.26].

Overpopulation and waste

Whatever the emissions or consumption of resources are or might be per capita, the totals will always be broadly in proportion to the global population which continues to increase and is currently close to seven billion [1.27]. In 1804 global population reached one billion for the first time, taking some 300 years to double from half a billion in 1500. Doubling has occurred again from 1804 to 1927 (123 years), from 1927 to 1974 (47 years) and almost certainly again by 2025 (51 years). By 2040 the world is likely to have around one and a half times as many people as it has today. As David Attenborough, respected natural-history film-maker and Patron of the Optimum Population Trust says, "I've never seen a problem that wouldn't be easier to solve with fewer people, or harder, and ultimately impossible, with more."

Such predictions of population vary with assumptions and one cannot rule out the effect of wars to secure scarce resources. Water is increasingly scarce and 60% of countries share a common river, lake or catchment area with other countries [1.5].

Food may become scarce too. A study of microscopic marine plants which are at the beginning of the food chain and fundamental to life in the oceans has detected a 40% decline in phytoplankton since 1950 [1.28]. This micro-organism is capable of photosynthesis and accounts for about half the organic matter on the Planet. It produces much of the oxygen we all need to breathe. A detailed study of ocean fish supplies predicts a total collapse by 2048 [1.29, 1.30] and Hudson Bay polar bears might soon be extinct, according to researchers from the University of Alberta, due to a steady annual reduction in sea ice which prevents them gaining access to food during the summer months [1.31]. Bees, so vital to pollinating crops, are in decline too [1.32].

Humans hardly help. Environmental gas flares in Nigeria are visible from space. Around 100 flares burn off gas continuously because the oil companies cannot find economically efficient ways to use it. Estimates of 30% to 40% of the energy available is wasted in this way. Some flares have been burning since the 1960s and a typical flare could supply power to 5000 homes. The flares production of CO_2 each year is equivalent to the pollution of eight million cars. The total waste in Nigeria is equivalent to 25% of the entire UK energy requirement and yet 60% of the Nigerian population has no access to a reliable supply of electricity [1.33]. Alongside this waste, oil companies nevertheless strive to find oil in increasingly difficult locations and to run risks which end in catastrophe. Witness BP's failure to have a prepared solution to a deep-sea drilling failure in the Gulf of Mexico in 2010. And, seemingly more modestly in comparison, the UK will run out of landfill in which to deposit annually 57 million tonnes of our rubbish by 2018 [1. 34].

We are assembling a recipe for 21st century pain and conflict. In the end, population may simply decline due to war, drought and famine.

Growth and debt

Meanwhile the UK continues to press for growth. This is partly to compensate for the fall in national output during 2008-10 of around 6% due to the recession [1.35] and partly because major banks have needed injections of public money to buy or re-capitalize them. And why, because banks are not just businesses but central to the operation of the capitalist system. Large banks cannot be allowed to fail it seems. They had firstly borrowed money which was in reality underwritten by close to worthless assets. They had then used these assets as collateral in further deals and in some cases continued the process of lending and borrowing to the point where debts were backed by as little as a thirtieth part of their notional value. The bubble burst when some investors called for a return of their loans which was of course impractical. Credit to fill the gap was simply not available once this was known.

A large slice of debt was (and still is) based on the so-called subprime mortgages. These are the aggregated loans to millions of individuals who purchase their homes and repay the capital and interest over many years. Unfortunately the credit worthiness of a large proportion of these individuals was so bad that they could not repay either interest or capital. Credit controls had been so weak and the financial incentives to sell credit so high, that mortgage debt had risen without check for more than a decade. Regulation clearly failed demonstrably badly in the USA [1.36, 1.37].

The explosion of risky investment not only dragged the global financial systems close to catastrophe but simultaneously inflated house prices so that the mortgages on them (purchase loans) cost more than the houses are now worth. Even those borrowers who are able to repay are repaying for loans which exceed the value of their property. Millions of people in the UK thus find themselves with negative equity of up to 16% and can only sell their houses at a loss [1.38, 1.39]. If any such borrower defaults the value of the house when sold will not cover the outstanding debt, a serious matter of concern for both the borrower AND the lender. Nonetheless, the banking system has made, and continues to make a few individuals very rich [1.40, 1.41 1.42,1.43].

Until July 2010 the UK Government public debt did not include its investment in the railway network and excluded public borrowing through private-finance-initiatives (PFI) and public-private-partnerships (PPP). It omitted the commitment to public-sector pensions which are funded via taxes by private-sector workers whose pensions are, on average, grossly inferior [1.44]. It fudged whether the amount of collateral owned by the banks, which have been bailed out by taxpayers to the tune of £50 billion in cash and a further £450 billion in various loan options and guarantees, were assets as repayable loans or debts to be written off. This was because of the opaqueness and complexity of the financial products which caused the calamity. Meanwhile, the UK national budget for 2010 includes a planned deficit of more than £155 billion, nearly £3000 per person including children, to add to the existing debt!

Something approaching the true UK position was revealed by the Office of National Statistics (ONS) in July 2010 [1.45] :

Future payments for the state, old age pension: *£1.1 trn*
to £1.4 trn
Unfunded public-sector pensions for teachers, NHS staff   *£770 bn*
to £1.2 trn
and civil servants
Payments under private finance initiatives (PFI)   *£200 bn*
Liabilities such as bank deposit guarantees   *£500 bn*
Nuclear power plant decommissioning   *£45 bn*
Impact of financial-sector interventions   *£1 trn*
to £1.5 trn

On these figures the total is around £3.8 trillion and represents one of the worst per capita indebtedness of any government in the developed world. It might be the worst but the basis for calculating any country's true indebtedness is not exact so comparisons are difficult. For example, immediately following the publication of the above by the ONS, the Institute of Economic Affairs (IEA) calculated the national debt to be closer to £4.8 trillion or £78,000 for every person in the UK. It claims this is largely because the state pension commitment had been under-estimated.

In addition, the total personal debt of UK residents is close to the UK's gross domestic product of just over £1.5 trillion and means that a quick exit from indebtedness is impractical. The UK population is so heavily in debt and burdened with interest repayments that it is unable to obtain further credit with which to spend. About 80% of the debt is for house mortgages and 20% for goods and services (credit-card debt). The debt has reduced the demand for products and services which was already inflated by credit-funded purchases over many years. Many companies, retailers in particular, thus have too much capacity and too many employees for current demand. It is a "double whammy" since (a) there is no longer the demand previously funded by debt, and (b) interest payments on would-be-purchasers' debts account for what ought to have been a contribution to the normal level of purchasing. Banks, for all their faults, cannot justify lending to companies which supply a market which has collapsed.

In a further attempt to stimulate economic activity and a return to growth, the Government has also issued bonds under a policy of "quantitative easing", that is printing new money. As of January 2010 some £200 billion had been issued which, if basic economic theory means anything, will lead to inflation of at least 10% sometime in the future.

So the Government is striving to inject money into the economy, the so-called fiscal stimulus, to promote purchasing. While one can see the political expediency of such fiscal stimulus, which is a reason but not necessarily a justification for it, the measures are an attempt to provide money for people to continue buying the products and services they cannot afford, to cover the excess capacity and pay employees. The hope (sic) is that growth will catch up meanwhile so that capacity and markets come into natural balance again before everyone has to pay for that unwanted capacity. As the Archbishop of Canterbury observed, "It's like giving a drug addict an incentive to increase his addiction". As Kenneth Boulding, environmental adviser to President Kennedy stated many years ago, "Anyone who believes in indefinite growth of anything physical on a finite planet is either a madman or an economist."

The national debt is mimicking that of its population. If it rises, seemingly out of control, to pay for goods and services the UK cannot afford, with money borrowed from prudent savers such as the Chinese and the oil and energy rich, how will we survive? Lenders may simply demand their money back, which would destroy the value of our currency, or we shall spend so much on interest and debt repayments that we will have nothing to pay for pensions, healthcare, social services and economic development. The USA is in a similar position and there is gathering concern that, in financial terms, it is actually tottering on the edge of a nuclear-scale catastrophe [1.46, 1.47]. The USA and UK owe far more than those African countries over which we fly with indifference, pity or scorn [1.48]. As Alan Greenspan, chairman from 1987 to 2006 of the United States Federal Reserve Board, which oversees the US Federal Reserve Bank, says, "Humans cannot survive unless they make some provision for the future".

Given that the root cause of the collapse is due to banks trading in dodgy assets on the back of Government policies which for many years were anything but prudent, one might reasonably ask whether assessing the risk of default by a repayment mortgage is especially difficult. Compare it for example with deciding whether a Boeing 777 airliner with 350 people on board is fit to fly to Johannesburg? Is it difficult when you can collect statistics to obtain rates of mortgage default? Such data can ensure that across all payments there is some provision to compensate for what are essentially predictable rates of loss. What is the problem when you know the price of the house, the earnings and prospects of the purchaser, projected interest rates and period of repayment?

Well of course there isn't a problem; a teenager with reasonable grades in mathematics should easily be able to do the calculations and those who work for banks are generally numerate and sufficiently qualified. It is thus hard to avoid the conclusion that those devising the "toxic" financial products and trading in them (both sellers and buyers) were simply negligent or fraudulent. And, here is another "crunch", would you travel on the Johannesburg flight if those bankers, or the government regulators employed to watch over them, were in charge of checking the aircraft?

Evolution or extinction

This then is the point referred to in my opening sentence and the reason for this book: technology delivering magic, capitalism festering from greed, everyone plundering the planet and its poorest suffering from our collective inadequacy. The UK is virtually bankrupt just when it needs the funds to reduce its emissions and tackle the effects of climate change. Its public-sector enjoys better remuneration than its private-sector, despite the need for the ideas, enterprise, innovation and drive of the latter to remedy its problems. Individuals feel impotent to change the system. Are we simply progressing towards extinction or evolving towards a better life? If extinction, what are the drivers and what might we do about them? This book is an engineer's attempt to try to make some sense of it.

Notes and references for Chapter 1

1.1 *The 555 seat Airbus A380-800, with a non-stop range of 8,000 nautical miles (14,800km), was launched in December 2000. The aircraft entered production in January 2002. Its first flight (with the Rolls-Royce engines) took place from Blagnac Airport, Toulouse, in April 2005 and its first commercial flight was by Singapore Airlines from Singapore to Sydney on 25 October 2007.*
The aircraft is equipped with four 70,000-pound thrust engines, either the Rolls-Royce Trent 900 or the General Electric / Pratt & Whitney Engine Alliance GP7200. There are ten fuel tanks with a capacity of 131,000 litres of fuel. Refuelling can be carried out in 40 minutes.
The aircraft has eight full-size doors on either side. On both sides two doors on the main deck and one door on the upper deck, forward of the wing, can be used simultaneously for embarking or disembarking passengers.
The take-off length is 2,900m at maximum weight at sea level, ISA +15° conditions and the initial cruise altitude 10,500 m. The aircraft complies with the noise emission limits of ICAO for overfly, approach and side-on manoeuvres and meets the stricter regulations of London Heathrow airport concerning take-off and landing. This enables aircraft operations at night.

1.2 *The Dreamliner, or Boeing 787 family of aircraft as it is officially called, is in the 200 to 300-seat class and will carry passengers non-stop on routes between 6,500km and 16,000km at speeds up to Mach 0.85. Aircraft assembly began in June 2006 and final assembly in May 2007. Its first flight was in 2009.*
The aircraft is broadly of conventional design with low sweptback wings and two underwing pylon mounted engines, either the General Electric GENX or the Rolls-Royce Trent 1000. Each type is capable of developing 55,000 to

70,000 pounds thrust. The design is unconventional in using lightweight, high durability composites and advanced aluminium alloys in the main structure. It is highly fuel-efficient and offers lower cost of travel in terms of seat cost per mile. It also has the ability to fly directly to smaller regional airports instead of to larger airports where passengers proceed to transfer flights to regional destinations.

1.3 *In his 2008 book "Blood River", Tim Butcher reports that the bloodiest war in the world, that in the Congo at the very heart of Africa, was seeing 1,000 deaths a day due to violence. It made the conflict in Afghanistan seem like a peaceful haven and yet the world hardly appeared to have noticed. In a review of the book, Lesley Mason says: " The phrase that stays in the mind long after closing the book is the concept that The Congo (by whatever name we choose to call it) is a country that is 'not just undeveloped but undeveloping'. The visions of railway lines being reclaimed by the jungle flora is a clear enough one for a country being reclaimed by the mores of an earlier age, a more violent age – an age when the world could not penetrate the depths or hope to influence what went on in the remoteness. The question is: are we (the richer world) prepared to allow that to continue, or do the people that Butcher met on his travels deserve a better future?"*
Butcher, Tim, *Blood River: A Journey to Africa's Broken Heart,* Chatto and Windus, 2008. ISBN-10: 0701179813, ISBN-13: 978-0701179816.

1.4 *A few statistics cannot remotely convey the suffering and the complexity of the issues which define human life in much of Africa, so the succinct nature of the following table may border on the obscene. Alternatively, on might feel that this same brevity lends them power. Just look at the figures for life expectancy and the GDP per capita and compare them to those for USA and UK.*

Country	Pop. Millions	GDP $ per capita	Life expectancy	External debt $ million
Angola	12.5	7,800	37.9	8,400
Central African Republic	4.4	700	44	1,150
DR Congo	66.5	300	54	10,000
Kenya	39.0	1600	54.7	6,700
Mozambique	21.3	800	41	4,189
Nigeria	146.3	2,100	46.5	8,000
Rwanda	10.2	80	49.8	1,400
Sierra Leone	6.3	600	41	1,610
Somalia	9.6	600	49.3	3,000
Sudan	40.2	1,900	50.3	29,400
Zimbabwe	11.35	200	44.3	5.16
UK	61	35,000	78.9	10,450,000* June 2007
USA	304	45,000	78.1	12,250,000 June 2007

* Dollars used for comparison purposes; value changes with £/$ exchange rate.

Source: The World Fact Book, CIA, USA.

The statistics do not convey the fact that in 2008 in Somalia, a 13-year-old girl was stoned to death for having been raped. During the war in Sierra Leone (1991-2002) both the arms were cut off thousands of individuals to leave them alive but in misery.

In March 2010, "The Times" reported that some 500 people including women and children were massacred by rampaging gangs in the city of Jos in Nigeria. The report states " ---- the limbs of slaughtered children (lay) tangled in a grotesque mess. One toddler appeared fixed in the protective but hopeless embrace of an older child, possibly his brother. Another had been scalped. Most had severed hands and feet."

Across central and west Africa albino-individuals are hunted and killed to provide body parts for adding potency to black-magic rituals. The Central African Republic is Africa's operational centre for trafficking children for sexual exploitation.

1.5 *At any one time:*
- *Half of the world's hospital beds are occupied by patients suffering from water-borne diseases.*
- *Over one-third of the world's population has no access to sanitation facilities.*
- *In developing countries, about 80% of illnesses are linked to poor water and sanitation conditions.*
- *One out of every four deaths under the age of 5 worldwide is due to a water-related disease.*
- *In developing countries, it is common for water collectors, usually women and girls, to have to walk several kilometres every day to fetch water. Once filled, pots and jerry cans weigh as much as 20kg (44lbs)*
- *Some 60% of countries share water resources with one or more other countries.*

Insights from the Comprehensive Assessment of Water Management in Agriculture, Stockholm World Water Week, International Water Management Institute (IWMI), 2006, Columbo, Sri Lanka.

1.6 *Economic scarcity of water occurs when there is a lack of investments in water or lack of human capacity to keep up with growing water demand. Much of the scarcity for people is due to the way institutions function, favouring* *one group over another, not hearing the voices of various groups, especially women. Symptoms of economic water scarcity include little (small or large) infrastructure development so that people have trouble getting enough water for agriculture or even drinking; or inequitable distribution of water even though infrastructure exists. Much of sub-Saharan Africa is characterized by economic scarcity, where further water development could ease poverty problems. Many small pockets exist throughout the globe where institutions struggle to equitably distribute resources.*

International Water Management Institute (IWMI), Columbo, Sri Lanka.

1.7 *According to figures released at the 2009 meeting of the G8 countries in Italy, the world's population is set to rise from 6.7 to 9.2 billion and Africa's starving to 600 million by 2050. Two thirds of the world's malnourished people currently live in only seven countries which by 2050 are destined to have another 1.1 billion. This accounts for almost 45% of global population growth. Experts say that increasing agricultural production is the only answer yet the world's efforts are directed at short-term food aid and relief. The UN estimates that around 1 billion people regularly go hungry and 3.2 million children die annually from malnutrition.*

See also Renewing American Leadership in the Fight Against Global Hunger and Poverty by Dan Glickman (the former U.S. Secretary of Agriculture) and Catherine Bertini (former Executive Director of the UN World Food Program), available online at www.thechicagocouncil.org/globalagdevelopment

1.8 *Airline emissions are 'far higher than previous estimates'. An unpublished study by the world's leading experts has revealed that airlines are pumping 20 per cent more carbon dioxide into the atmosphere than estimates suggest, with total emissions set to reach between 1.2 billion and 1.5 billion tonnes annually by 2025. The report, which is by the US Department of Transport, the European air traffic management body, Eurocontrol, Manchester Metropolitan University and the technology company QinetiQ, predicts that airline CO_2 emissions will rise from the current level of 670 million tonnes to up to 1.48 billion tonnes by 2025. This exceeds the previous estimate, made in 2004, of 1.03 billion tonnes by 2025. The growth in aviation CO_2 means that the highest forecast for aviation emissions produced by the International Panel on Climate Change will be met or exceeded.*

Cahal Milmo in *The Independent*, 6th May, 2008

1.9   Rolls-Royce has developed the Trent family of large turbofans. These Trent engines carry advanced technology features and are designed to have a minimum impact on the environment. The Boeing 777, which is powered by two Trent 800 engines, carries around 330 passengers and gives about 120 passenger-miles to the gallon. This is equivalent to a family-sized car with three occupants travelling at 40 miles per hour at 40 miles per gallon. However, the Boeing 777 travels 10 times faster.

1.10   In July 2008 the European Parliament voted in favour of including airline emissions in the EU Emissions Trading System. From 2012 all flights within, to or from the EU will be included in the trading scheme. So airlines will either be able to sell their allowances if they do not use them or will have to purchase more if they emit more than expected. From 2012 airline emissions will have to be 97 per cent of what they were as an average between 2004 and 2006, falling to 95 per cent in 2013. But 85 per cent of allowances will be free to start with.

1.11   According to meteorologists the 2005 average global temperature equalled (within several hundredths of a degree) the record warm year of 1998. Years 2002-4 and 2006-7 were nearly as warm. The 12 warmest years on record have all occurred since 1990. www.worldviewofglobalwarming.org

1.12   A study by scientists from the US National Snow and Ice Data Centre (NSIDC) in Colorado has confirmed that Arctic amplification, that the Arctic will warm at a faster rate than the rest of the world ,is occurring several decades earlier than predicted.
According to Dr Julienne Stroeve of the NSIDC, "The warming climate is leading to more open water in the Arctic Ocean. As these open water areas develop through spring and summer, they absorb most of the sun's energy, leading to ocean warming. In autumn, as the sun sets in the Arctic, most of the heat that was gained in the ocean during summer is released back to the atmosphere, acting to warm the atmosphere. It is this heat-release back that gives us Arctic amplification". Temperature readings for October 2008 were significantly higher than normal across the entire Arctic region – between 3°C and 5°C above average – but some areas were dramatically higher. In the Beaufort Sea, north of Alaska, for instance, near-surface air temperatures were more than 7°C higher than normal for the time of year.
Computer models have predicted ice-free summers in the Arctic by 2070 but this recent evidence points to the possibility of these occurring by 2030.

1.13 *Researchers at NOAA's National Climate Data Centre (NCDC) have found evidence that the rate of global warming is accelerating and that in the past 25 years it achieved the rate of two degrees Celsius (four degrees Fahrenheit) per century. This rate had previously been predicted for the 21st Century. www.sciencedaily.com/releases/2000/02/000222103553.htm*

1.14 *Climate change is a more dangerous threat to society than terrorism, according to Professor Sir David King, UK Government Chief Scientist in 2007.*

1.15 *The chart below shows the historic and projected summer temperature anomaly in Europe over time, as calculated using simulations of all the planetary, volcanic and industrial factors which affect it. It also shows the historic record of measured temperature over time. Since the historical record of actual and simulated temperatures from 1900 to 2003 are in reasonable agreement, it is the widely accepted hypothesis that the predicted values are likely to be correct too. Thus the high temperatures of 2003 are predicted to become the average within 40 years and a six-degree rise probable within 90.*

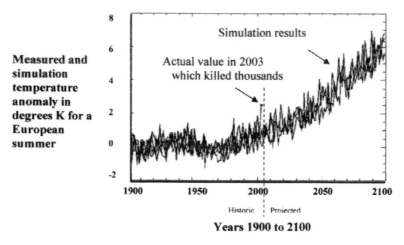

Years 1900 to 2100

Source: Peter Stott, Hadley Centre   © Crown Copyright 2004, the Met Office

1.17   New research by the University of East Anglia (UEA) has demonstrated for the first time that human activity is responsible for significant warming in both polar regions. Updated data-sets of land surface temperatures and simulations from four new climate models show that temperature rises in both polar regions are not consistent with natural climate variability alone and are directly attributable to human influence.

Previous studies have observed rises in both Arctic and Antarctic temperatures over recent decades but have not formally attributed the changes to human influence due to poor observation data and large natural variability. Moreover, the International Panel on Climate Change (IPCC) had concluded that Antarctica was the only continent where human-induced temperature changes had yet to be detected.

The results demonstrate that human activity has already caused significant warming, with impacts on polar biology, indigenous communities, ice-sheet mass balance and global sea level.

Gillett, Nathan et al., *Attribution of polar warming to human influence,* Nature Geoscience, *30th October, 2008.*

The authors of the article include Nathan Gillett (UEA/Environment Canada), Phil Jones (UEA), Alexey Karpechko (UEA), Daithi Stone (University of Oxford/Tyndall Centre for Climate Change Research), Peter Scott (Met Office Hadley Centre), Toru Nozawa (National Institute for Environmental Studies, Japan), Gabriele Hegerl (University of Edinburgh), and Michael Wehner (Lawrence Berkeley National Laboratory, California).

1.18   The Sun heats the tropics much more than the polar regions, but the resulting extremes of temperature are moderated by compensating heat circulation in the atmosphere and the ocean. Most notably, warm upper water, referred to as the Gulf Stream or Atlantic Conveyor, intrudes far into the northern North Atlantic. It brings warmth to Northern Europe and saves the UK in particular from the low temperatures found at similar latitudes in Canada, Russia and China. If this transfer of heat should cease then UK winter temperatures would be much lower and pack ice would form around the coast for several months each year. Construction, housing, heating systems and transport would need to change dramatically to enable citizens to cope with extra "cold" rather than extra "hot". Addressing this concern, computer simulations predict that global warming will weaken the ocean circulation that transports heat from the tropics to higher latitudes in the North Atlantic. Such an effect has now been practically detected in the Gulf Stream.

Detlef Quadfase, Nature 438, 565-566, December, 2005.

1.19   *In June, 2008:*
Mark Serreze of the US National Snow and Ice Data Centre(NSIDC) in Colorado said "For the first time that I am aware of, the North Pole is covered with extensive first-year ice – ice that formed last autumn and winter. I'd say that it's even-odds on whether the North Pole melts out."
Dr Ron Lindsay, a polar scientist at the University of Washington in Seattle agrees, saying,"There's a good chance that it will all melt away at the North Pole, it's certainly feasible, but it's not guaranteed."
Professor Peter Wadhams of Cambridge University, who was one of the first civilian scientists to sail underneath the Arctic sea ice in a Royal Navy submarine, says, "The conditions are ripe for an unprecedented melting of ice at the North Pole. The ice has been getting thinner – a change of 40% in the past 20 years. Sea ice has a rugged underside with deep pressure ridges pushing blocks of ice down 50 metres or more. These are disappearing, there are only a quarter as many as there were 20 years ago."
Scientists at the Nasa Goddard Space Flight Centre say that the "polynya", an area of open water surrounded by sea ice that forms annually near Alaska and Banks Island, off the Canadian coast, is much larger than normal.

1.20   *In July 2009:*
The seasonal extent of Arctic sea ice declined at an average rate of 97,000 km² (37,000 square miles) per day. This decline was faster than in 2008 when it was 87,000 km² (34,000 square miles) per day, but slower than in 2007, when ice extent declined at a rate of 111,000 km² (43,000 square miles) per day.
US National Snow and Ice Data Centre. *http://nsidc.org/*

1.21   *Screen, J.A. and Simmonds, I., The central role of diminishing sea ice in recent Arctic temperature amplification,* Nature, 464, 1334-1337, 2010.

1.22   *A series of expeditions led by Igor Semlitov of the Russian Academy of Sciences has detected a steady increase in the methane emissions from sub-sea deposits of the gas which are normally sealed in by ice or permafrost. Since 2003 the expeditions have detected a number of methane hotspots where chimneys of methane are bubbling to the surface at more than 100 times the background level.*

1.23   Corinne Le Quéré, Michael R. Raupach, Josep G. Canadell, Gregg Marland et al., *Trends in the sources and sinks of carbon dioxide,* Nature Geoscience **2**, 831 – 836, 2009.

1.24   *The global average temperature will increase by 2°C to 3°C this century according to mid-range estimates by the Intergovernmental Panel on Climate Change (IPCC). This rise in temperature means that the Earth will experience a greater climate change than it has for at least 10,000 years and it will be difficult for many people and ecosystems to adapt to this rapid change.*
The temperature increases are likely to result in an increased frequency and severity of weather events such as heat waves, storms and flooding. Rising levels of greenhouse gases in the atmosphere could set in motion large-scale changes in the Earth's natural systems. Some of these could be irreversible. The melting of large ice sheets will result in major consequences for low-lying areas throughout the world.
www.metoffice.gov.uk/climatechange/guide/keyfacts

1.25   *To constrain global warming to within 2°C, developed countries would need to cut their emissions to 25–40 per cent below 1990 levels by 2020 and to 50–80 per cent below 1990 levels by 2050, according to the best available scientific analyses. Most developed countries (referred to as Annex I parties under the UN Framework Convention on Climate Change (UNFCCC) have specific proposals, domestic policy processes or a clear intent expressed at high political levels from which the amount of ambition for Copenhagen in terms of emissions reductions in 2020 can be inferred. A number of countries have also stated their positions on reducing greenhouse gas emissions by 2050. Many developing countries — including Brazil, China, India and South Africa, whose combined greenhouse gas emissions in 1990 and 2005 amounted, respectively, to 58 and 60 per cent of non-Annex I emissions — have climate policies in place or have declared their intent to adopt policies with sufficient clarity to enable an estimate of their future emissions.*
The current best "Halfway to Copenhagen" pathway has virtually no chance of limiting warming to 2°C (or 1.5°C) above pre-industrial temperatures — or, put another way, it is virtually certain to exceed 2 °C.
Joeri Rogelj, Bill Hare, Julia Nabel, Kirsten Macey, Michiel Schaeffer, Kathleen Markmann and Malte Meinshausen, *Halfway to Copenhagen, no way to 2°C,* Nature Reports Climate Change, published online 11th June, 2009.

1.26   According to a study by Professor Pierre Friedlingstein and others, the planet may reach record levels of emissions by the end of 2010. During 2009, in a period of global recession, CO_2 emissions fell as economic activity slowed, but since then the world has shown modest signs at recovery. The pace of economic activity has picked up and so have global CO_2 emissions. They are set to reach record levels by the end of 2010.
The Universities of Exeter and of East Anglia and other international institutions took part in the study which is part of the Global Carbon Project which records annual totals of CO_2 greenhouse gas emissions.
www.globalcarbonproject.org/carbonbudget

1.27   World Population to 2300, United Nations, Department of Economic and Social Affairs, 2004.

1.28   Daniel G. Boyce, Marlon R. Lewis and Boris Worm, Global phytoplankton decline over the past century, **Nature, 466, 29ᵗʰ July, 2010.**

1.29   Ransom A. Myers and Boris Worm, Rapid world-wide depletion of predatory fish communities, Nature 423, 15ᵗʰ May, 2003.

1.30   A film documentary in which scientists predict that if we continue fishing as we are now, we will see the end of most seafood by 2048. The documentary chronicles how demand for cod off the coast of Newfoundland in the early 1990s led to the decimation of the most abundant cod population in the world, how hi-tech fishing vessels leave no escape routes for fish populations and how farmed fish as a solution is a myth. It lays the responsibility squarely on consumers who innocently buy endangered fish, politicians who ignore the advice and pleas of scientists, fishermen who break quotas and fish illegally, and the global fishing industry that is slow to react to an impending disaster.
The End of the Line, Sundance Film Festival, Utah, January, 2009.

1.31   Péter K. Molnár, Andrew E. Derocher, Gregory W. Thiemann and Mark A. Lewis, Predicting survival, reproduction and abundance of polar bears under climate change, Biological Conservation, Volume 143, Issue 7, July, 2010.

1.32   A film highlighting the problem and mystery of why billions of bees are disappearing due to "colony collapse disorder".
George Langworthy and Maryam Henein, *Vanishing of the bees,* 2009.

1.33   Visible from space, deadly on Earth: the gas flares of Nigeria, Daniel Howden in *The Independent,* 27ᵗʰ April, 2010.

1.34   Gary Porter, Chairman of the (UK) Local Government Association, July, 2010.

1.35   National Institute of Social and Economic Research (NIESR), January, 2010.

1.36   The collapse of Lehman came after the US Treasury refused to bail out the embattled 158-year-old bank, a crucial shift after its support in March 2008 for a Wall Street rescue of failing Bear Stearns. Lehman was felled by the weight of about $60 billion in toxic bad debts. It went under holding assets of $639 billion against debts of $613 billion. The Times, 16ᵗʰ September, 2008.

1.37   Regulation failed to prevent Bernard Madoff from carrying out a $50 billion "Ponzi Scheme" fraud even though Harry Markopolos, a Boston accountant, had discovered it in 2000 and reported it to the Securities and Exchange Commission (SEC). He has been jailed for 150 years. At $50 billion, the fraud is more than twenty times the GDP of Zimbabwe.

1.38   In June 2009, Northampton was the negative equity capital of Britain with a value of 16.9%. Ipswich was in tenth place with 13.1%. Although Scotland recorded only 3.6%, East Midlands, East Anglia and Yorkshire and Humber averaged more than 13%. Fitch Ratings, 2009.

1.39   Repossession figures published in February 2010, report that 46,000 repossessions were made in 2009, up 15% from 2008 and that 188,000 homeowners were currently in arrears by more than 2.5%. UK Council for Mortgage Lenders, 2010.

1.40   US financier Warren Buffet has a personal fortune of $62 billion which is sufficient to pay the state pension of a UK citizen for eight million years or eight million pensioners for one year.

1.41   Annual bonuses paid by major banks and financial services companies in the City of London reached £12 billion a year in 2007. This is sufficient to fund a million small businesses with £12,000 each or, to compensate the anticipated UK's three million unemployed by the end of 2010 with £4000 per person. Large bonuses for senior managers and directors have continued despite the large subsidies by taxpayers in both the UK and US, in 2008, 2009 and 2010.

1.42 *The remuneration of the leaders of two of the banks which have received massive injections of taxpayers' money was:*

- *Andy Hornby, former chief executive of HBOS: annual salary £940,000 plus £700,000 bonus Lord Stevenson of Coddenham, former chairman of HBOS: remuneration £821,000 in 2007*
- *Sir Fred Goodwin, former chief executive of RBS: salary £4,200,000 in 2007 plus £2,800,000 bonus and 695,188 shares.*
- *Sir Tom McKillop, former chairman of RBS: remunerations £750,000 in 2007.*

1.43 *When Richard Fuld, head of Lehman Brothers, faced questioning from the U.S. House of Representatives Committee on Oversight and Government Reform, Henry Waxman asked, "Your company is now bankrupt, our economy is in crisis, but you get to keep $480 million.*
I have a very basic question for you, is this fair?" Fuld said that he had in fact taken about $300 million in pay and bonuses over the past eight years. Despite Fuld's defence on his high pay, Lehman Brothers executive pay was reported to have increased significantly before filing for bankruptcy.

1.44 *The UK government is facing calls to reveal the true cost of public sector pensions after it emerged that they may be worth more than 15 times those of private sector workers.*
Opposition politicians and business leaders have joined forces with the CBI employers' body in demanding an independent investigation into the generous final salary pensions awarded to millions of civil servants, NHS workers and teachers at an estimated cost of up to £one trillion to the taxpayer.
The average public sector worker will be entitled to a pension worth £17,091 a year, according to data compiled by Ros Altmann, a former adviser to Tony Blair. By contrast, the average private sector pension annuity last year paid £1,086.
The Taxpayers' Alliance has obtained figures showing that 17,150 public sector workers have already retired with pension pots worth more than £one million each. Nearly 10,500 NHS workers; 3,680 civil servants; 815 judges; 1,800 teachers, mainly former heads; and 167 Royal Mail staff have retired on seven-figure pension funds.

It says council taxpayers in England and Wales are each contributing an average £226 towards the pensions of local government workers. However, the BBC and the parliamentary pensions fund refused to release figures of how many retired staff and MPs have £one million pension pots.

Generous pensions have traditionally been regarded as a necessary for public sector workers, who in the past commanded lower pay than the private sector. But under the Labour Government, public sector earnings have overtaken the private sector.

According to the Office for National Statistics, the average public sector worker earned £25,896 a year in 2007, compared to £22,828 in the private sector. Only the top 20% of private sector workers are paid more than public sector peers.

Altmann said: "Public sector pensions are now being propped up by Alice in Wonderland economics." It would cost £427,275 to buy an annuity delivering the average public sector pension of £17,091 from an insurance firm. The Association of British Insurers said that the average private sector pension pot used to purchase an annuity in the UK last year was just £24,150.

Philip Hammond, shadow chief secretary to the Treasury, said: "The growing gap between public and private sector pensions is creating an apartheid which is unhealthy in society and damaging to our economy. We need an open debate about the scale of public sector pension liabilities."

In 2006 the government raised the retirement age of new entrants to public sector pensions schemes and made a series of other changes in a bid to reduce its pension costs by £13bn. These reforms will only cut its pension bill by 1% over the next 50 years."

Robert Watts in *The Sunday Times*, 2nd November, 2008.

1.45   Office of National Statistics, July, 2010.

1.46   *"Politicians do not know what to do about it (the fiscal time bomb)", says David Walker, Comptroller General of the USA from 1998 to 2008. He has resigned his position and now leading a "Fiscal Wake-up Tour" in the US which includes organisations such as "The Concord Coalition" and "Concerned Youth of America". The objective is to bring the attention of the population and politicians that they are living beyond their means; that the fiscal facts are not political statements but alarming facts. Among which are:*

- *US citizens are now spending more than they earn, a savings rate of -2.9%*
- *The US trade balance is the largest in the world at $816 billion in 2007*
- *The 2008 federal budget contains a deficit of $602 billion so even current plans increase the national debt*

- *While the official federal debt is around $10 trillion and bad enough, the hidden commitments to Medicare and other federal obligations means the real figure is closer to $53 trillion; $170,000 per citizen.*

1.47 Peter G. Peterson, *Running on Empty: How the Democratic and Republican Parties Are Bankrupting Our Future and What Americans Can Do about It,* Farrar, Straus and Giroux, New York, 2004 ISBN-10: 0-374-25287-4, ISBN-13: 0-374-25287-8.

1.48 *Given that the global population is around six billion people and the combined gross national product of all the world's countries is $55 trillion, the average annual income per head is approximately $9000. If a viable socio-economic group is two adults and two children, what we would traditionally call a nuclear family, it could arithmetically receive $36,000 dollars (Warren Buffet thus already has enough for nearly two million such families). While admitting that the complexities of what exactly GDP consists of besides incomes, and the need to differentiate payments to individuals to provide incentives and reward them for hard work, special skills and outstanding contributions to their fellow beings, this isn't so far from being an income which could sustain everyone and be sustainable for the planet (probably more than sufficient but that's an educated guess).*
It is obviously an oversimplification but shows that if we settled for spreading out money more equitably, and addressed what we need to do to survive climate change, humankind is not very far from being able to occupy the planet in a truly sustainable fashion.

Chapter 2:
Evolution and survival

"Evolution ... is – a change from an indefinite, incoherent homogeneity, to a coherent heterogeneity."

Hebert Spencer (1820-1901)

Do we know enough about evolution to ensure the survival of our species? Some kind of answer may lie in the nature of evolution as revealed by the theories of Ashby, Darwin, Koestler, Lovelock, Malthus and Popper.

Context

Living memory is relatively short but I can stretch it a bit by recalling my youth and the world described by my forebears. My grandfather chauffeured the first private Rolls Royce motor car to visit continental Europe, yet his travels around his native Yorkshire were surprisingly constrained. The wheel base of the Rolls was so long that he had to avoid routes where the car would otherwise have grounded itself on the hump of a bridge. On one of his drives he recalls a visit to the opera by Tzar Nicholas. Some Russian with a dancing bear was entertaining the crowd and on seeing the Tzar, the man rushed forward to kiss the ground where HE had stepped, God's divine presence on Earth.

In his youth in the 1890s, letters might well have taken days to get to just one person in the next village. Today the same text can be delivered globally, to millions simultaneously and within seconds. Even more importantly most people can now read and write. Mister Nicholson, owner-manager of Nicholson's brewery in Maidenhead, where my other grandfather worked as a boy, no longer stands at his company's gate at 6.00 am to check the arrival of his employees. I doubt they would doff their caps nowadays as they did then. Caps are rarely needed and beer is no longer delivered by drays within the few miles a horse can cover in one day. All the breweries on the Thames have been bought by large corporations or closed. Maidenhead is now chock-a-block with traffic, marketing and information-technology companies and the smart residences of London's commuter belt.

We can look back earlier still to when the Snots lived as troglodytes beneath what is now called Nottingham and my adopted home (Snottingham is the original name so one can appreciate the change!). The caves are still in use as constant-temperature storage space but the tribal structure has long disappeared. Today we have a mix of local and national democracy with significant influence from the European Union and a sprinkling of quangos. Along the way we have endured a variety of socio-political structures in which tribes grew and merged to form kingdoms across the whole of the British Isles. These in turn were progressively reduced by a process of war, negotiation and marriage to the kingdoms of Scotland and England and finally the UK and the European Union itself.

Meanwhile, as history shows, the common man advanced slowly. Advanced may not be wholly accurate since tribal life may well have been preferable to the serfdom of the middle ages when, aside from punitive taxes, it was not unusual to have to drop everything to walk hundreds of miles to fight for some king with little shelter, food or proper weapons. Certainly the lot of the common man has changed since then. Significantly "man" now includes "woman" and in Europe both have equal rights under the law. In the UK less than 2% of people work in agriculture but 80% work in services. Employment in agriculture, the heavy industries and basic manufacturing are well past their peaks of the 19th and 20th centuries. Today, many of us earn a living from the professions, high-value manufacturing, design, retail and financial services, using intellectual or managerial rather than physical skills. Employment is mostly in very small companies, very large transnational companies or charities, the voluntary and public sectors. Medium-sized companies serving a particular geographic area have largely disappeared. Transnational companies can now outperform them through economies of scale, better service, better quality and lower prices.

So, homo sapiens, which as a species has scarcely changed physiologically for at least thirty millennia, has clearly adapted to enormous changes in lifestyle, opportunities and aspirations. The greatest change has been in the last 150 years, just the memory span of my extended family, and it seems to be accelerating.

More generally, the harnessing of energy, development of new materials and exploitation of semi-conductor technology, are demonstrably major contributors to the rising prosperity which industrialised nations have enjoyed in those 150 years. They have had a significant impact on political and economic thinking everywhere. Harnessing sources of energy has improved productivity and facilitated the international transport of people and goods. Electronics has delivered low-cost computation, information and communications technology (ICT). This too has similarly improved productivity and the dissemination of information and knowledge. Many intellectual skills are now embedded in software packages and made available to those who though less intellectually able can use them to widen their application and the delivery of benefits. Speed, convenience, accessibility and ease of reproduction at low labour and financial costs have ensured their uptake and success. They sustain, and are the engine of, the global economy. Indeed, a feature of the information revolution is the commoditization of knowledge.

In Europe, developments in energy and communications have coincided with an unprecedented period of international stability. This has almost certainly contributed to that stability in providing employment and an almost insatiable requirement for education and training. The Berlin wall was demolished and with it went the controlled-economic, socio-political systems of extreme socialism. Even the so-called underdeveloped nations, with few exceptions, have accepted a demand-led, free-market approach which, aided by improved communications and transport, has in turn delivered global markets and businesses. In the developed nations of the Americas and Europe, the great mass of working people have accumulated significant wealth. Governments and businesses have discovered that the buying power of the people (in the market place) is just as important as their productivity (in manufacturing and services). The acquisition of wealth, that is anything to which can be attributed monetary value, is the universal goal. Capitalism is accepted as fundamental to the human race and the driver of progress.

The past 25 years in particular illustrate a development of capitalism and a concern for national and even trans-national economic strategies. The World Trade Organization (WTO) and the creation of free-trade areas are attempts to cope with globalization, increasingly competitive markets and the emergence of the so-called BRIC nations (Brazil, Russia,

India and China) as industrial powers. In their economic strategies, ICT, biotechnology and other innovations which create and sustain employment and wealth, are greatly prized. This is also true in the hitherto developed economies which are losing many of their traditional manufacturing and location-independent service industries to these BRIC economies which can now do these same things very well but at lower-labour costs. The European Union is moving ever closer to a common currency and interest rate (even the UK considers adopting the Euro from time to time), which encourages and facilitates the movement of labour and investment. Migrants with a strong work ethic are taking up the more menial work (and relatively low paid jobs) in the developed countries because to them the earnings are high and they can establish platforms for a more ambitious future.

Simultaneously China and India are industrializing at a tremendous rate, building power stations and consuming fossil fuel in the traditional ways and exacerbating global warming [2.1]; difficult to criticize when the same approach remains the basis for the developed world's success and enviable standard of living. (By the way, there are some 2000 Chinese students currently studying at Nottingham's two universities and the University of Nottingham has campuses in China and Malaysia.) The population of the developed world is now highly familiar with the internet and personal computers at home and at work. This increasing ease with which any one person in whatever corner of the world can communicate largely unimpeded and uncontrolled with any other, has huge implications for how different cultures organize themselves. Terrorism is a major concern and the internet a significant help to terrorists and freedom fighters (take your pick) whether for propaganda purposes or to support and organize their dispersed followers. And, as if to increase the challenge, oil and sunshine, two of the principal sources of energy, are abundant in those areas which are least-stable, -predictable or -democratic.

These observations raise serious questions about how we overcome poverty while accepting free-market economics and how we reconcile economic imperatives with the environmental and social ones. For example, is capitalism itself part of the problem? What is certain is that technology will have a role in answering them. So too will what has been a parallel and major change in the paradigm which has dominated thinking in the developed world for more than 300 years; reductionism has now been joined by a healthy respect for holism. Complexity, chaos and fuzzy logic, which bear on our understanding of the animate as well as physical aspects of how our world ticks, are now considered worthy subjects for attention and have advanced considerably in recent decades [2.2, 2.3, 2.4].

So, quite simply, where is all this leading and will we continue to adapt successfully?

Darwin's theory

An obvious starting point is Darwin's theory of evolution since it is about the birth, development and survival of species, how they come about and how they survive. Although still a theory it is widely accepted by scientists and may simply be stated as a process of variation, whereby new forms are produced, followed by a process of selection whereby these new forms are evaluated to determine which shall survive [2.5].

Darwin's theory is commonly referred to as "the survival of the fittest" although this is strictly an incomplete statement because it ignores the primary process of variation.

Evolution is evident everywhere. Some people are active drivers of evolutionary change; those for example who successfully seek out variations in dogs, racehorses, pigeons and the like to selectively breed those with characteristics which favour speed and endurance so that they win races. Witness the amazing variety of species of dog, from poodles to miniatures, from dachunds to bulldogs. All have evolved through selective breeding from wolves in less than 1000 years. There are others who do similar things with farm animals to improve yields of milk, wool and meat, since industry and commerce are constantly trying to find new products and ways of doing business. These processes may be forced but they lead to evolution and can change a species quite rapidly. In the sub-world of viruses, new strains evolve at rates which mean we can expect a new type of 'flu each year and consequently need to re-vaccinate the old and vulnerable with a new and appropriate strain every winter. Evolution surrounds us.

So, what is the process of variation and what is the likely range of variety it might produce? Darwin himself was not clear what the precise mechanism might be although he perceived that reproduction is a prior requisite. Today we have a better understanding of the mechanism especially for the biological world. Research has revealed (a) that chromosomes, genes and DNA determine animal forms, (b) that mutations naturally occur in genetic structures, and (c) chromosomes combine and mix at reproduction

29

to create new structures. Furthermore, while mutation was long thought to be the driver for variety, it is the restructuring which appears to have the greatest effect since, unlike mutations, it occurs at every reproduction – very frequently.

Complex organisms carry between 10,000 and 100,000 genes [2.6]. If each gene has two alles then 2 to the power 10,000 or around 10 to the power 3,000 (a 1 followed by three thousand zeros) possible organisms could be produced. You are different to me precisely because of this fact and the occurrence of human forms such as Newton, Einstein, Kant, Hitler, Faraday and Genghis Khan are witness to examples of variety which were each capable of making a significant impact in their niche. Over time each species thus evolves or dies. So those with an inclination towards Hitler have digressed, those with an aptitude to understand and apply Newton have progressed, at least for the moment. All of geological time has not yet been sufficient to explore the total range of potential forms and the relatively small range of forms that have appeared since the beginning of time is thus easily explained.

Three implications spring immediately from these observations:
- There would seem to be no case for assuming a permanent equilibrium of species because there are so many possibilities it is impractical to predict what they might be, let alone how they might interact.
- The future is, for all practical purposes, unknowable since we do not know what future species will emerge (even before the selection process is brought to bear).
- When examining population genetics it is not sufficient to simply consider the struggle among existing forms since the generation of new forms is an important influence on outcomes. (This is a major factor in the analogy with organisational development.)

These bring us to the second component, the process of selection and its potential effect on our own survival? What are the limitations on the variety created?

Well, consider a hypothetical new form which has a survival advantage over the previous form of 5%. Over 400 generations with this advantage of 1.05/1 the new form would achieve a 250,000/1 superiority in number of progeny. Given that there are limitations in resources such as food, drink and shelter, the one with the larger progeny will therefore eventually displace the other and survive at its expense. As an example, the grey squirrel was introduced into the UK in 1876. It has progressively displaced the red squirrel which has disappeared from much of the UK. Only 140,000 or so remain, mostly north of the border with Scotland. The grey squirrel has meanwhile spread widely and numbers around 2.5 million.

The planet hosts at least a million species and scientists estimate that these represent the surviving 1% of all species that have ever existed. Paradoxically, scientists have also found evidence in fossils that some of the surviving species have existed for a very long time. So how do so many successfully compete, survive and coexist in a finite environment? The answer seems to be a combination of niches and adaptability.

Niches represent variations in the environment in which species exist and evolve. The most obvious are the physical niches created by climate and geology such as deserts, rain forests and swamps. But they also include the features in the wider environment as occupied by the existing species and including the behaviours of those species. Thus humans survive with relative ease in temperate climates with an abundance of water, food and shelter and few predators. Humans tend not to survive in climatic extremes where resources are scarce and predators, bacteria, poisonous snakes and other hazards compete for those same resources. A reason for the large number of species is therefore the existence of many niches which each provide survival opportunities for some of them. The reason for some species having survived for millions of years is that they adapted to their environments at an early stage and have proven to be the fitter of any subsequent variants which might have arisen in their environment.

In addition, evolution more generally seems to proceed by a process of variation in which small changes make a species fitter to occupy a niche than previously. Large changes of form mostly create species which are ill-suited to the niche in which they find themselves and die. Most critical of all is the fact that as this process of becoming fitter proceeds, the very nature of the niche and hence the wider environment, also changes. It is not as if evolution were an attempt to produce an optimal solution for a fixed environment but rather a continuous adjustment, through random variation and subsequent selection, to adapt to an ever changing world. Adaptability is thereby achieved implicitly by the process of evolution. What makes humans rather special (in scope and scale but not totally unique) is that they have an inbuilt skill, a feature of the species per se, which gives them the ability to adapt independently as it were, of evolution.

The human species does not have to wait for the evolutionary process to provide the adaptations needed to survive in a given niche, so long as the changes required by the changing niche are within the range for which the skill is adequate. For instance, humans can build houses in the Antarctic which protect them from both the cold and polar bears, use submersibles to enter the depths of the oceans and fly to the moon.

These observations do not preclude the evolution of the human race contributing further changes to the species which adapt it even more effectively for survival. Nor do they preclude the human race encountering conditions for which its own adaptability and any evolution-inspired changes all turn out to be inadequate. Crucially, they do not preclude human individuals and their progeny evolving with features that lead to dominance within the species itself (Hitler and Einstein etc.).

Because each one of us humans is different, just one of the ten to the power three thousand possibilities referred to above, we are individually an evolutionary step. Some feature in our genetic makeup might become reinforced by breeding with others to gain advantage in the niche around us. Or, we might already have features which give us a survival advantage in our niche.

If climate change continues apace, which of us will turn out to have the features to aid survival. Would it be those who have a genetic disposition to be able to manipulate others, apply technology, to lead, to collaborate, to be ruthless or whatever. In the 2009 Darwin Lecture at Cambridge, Professor John Dupre suggested that collaboration is a particularly important feature of evolution, a point with which this book is very much in sympathy. Or maybe it would be something purely physiological, like an ability to survive high temperatures or polluted air. If, by some chance, running twelve miles in under 60 minutes were a survival criterion we would see few Europeans and many more Africans in tomorrow's world.

Maybe those who currently wield most power will be the survivors because they can purchase the means to survive. Who knows? What is abundantly clear is that for all practical purposes the niche in which most of us are now challenged to survive has, until recently, been determined by their ability to contribute to capitalism. Capitalism has been our accepted niche for at least two hundred years. It is the period during which technology has enabled the majority of people in the developed world to operate largely without fear of starvation, premature death or disease. One is employed for a salary, in receipt of a pension or benefits. We are all consumers. There are no seriously tenable options for any individual in the developed world. One may thus put the hypothesis that our species has unconsciously created a niche which is largely independent of the natural world and so powerful that for most practical purposes it defines Darwin's process of human selection and possibly that of other species too. As already indicated in Chapter 1, the demand and economic drive for cheaper food has led to a depletion of global fish stocks and probable reduction in the numbers of bees which are needed to fertilize many crops. Phosphorous is an essential component of crop fertilizers and has no substitute. It is essential for the production of food and critical to feeding the expanding global population. Yet, there may be only 250 years of readily accessible supplies [2.7]. Oil and other fossil-fuel resources are obviously decreasing. Even though new sources are being discovered the Planet's reserves are getting smaller and to reduce emissions we shouldn't be using them anyway.

Beyond Darwin

Darwin's hypothesis is not the only scientific one on evolution. It is just one of five other complementary ideas or insights which are worthy of comment.

The first is due to one of the 20th century's most celebrated philosophers, Karl Popper. He has set out a complementary view to that encapsulated in "the survival of the fittest". Popper believed that Darwin's ideas had come to be interpreted as a process of conflict in which each evolutionary form struggled with a fundamentally hostile environment (the total environment consisting of the physical environment and the characteristics of other forms occupying the niche); that evolution was a process in which environments eliminated unsuitable forms and that those forms were essentially passive in an externally imposed selection process. In contrast to this last point, Popper believed that each evolutionary form was also active and driven from within to search for a better life and to find niches favourable to its own survival. He believed that life at all levels consists in the pursuit of a better life and problem solving [2.8].

The second has emerged more recently from Lovelock as Gaia theory [2.9]. This postulates that life and evolution are one and the same; that whatever form we take and however much we try individually to survive in our niches, we are simply part of a larger process of interconnected, interacting processes which will continue to live and evolve regardless of our success or failure. This has major implications for the widespread religious belief that man is something special in the universe whereby the world, including women, was created for man's benefit. The Gaia concept is that man is simply an integral, component part of the world and whether or not mankind survives a mere detail in the bigger picture. This is difficult for many to accept. Gaia is nonetheless a very plausible hypothesis and the principles well supported by others. Its key mechanisms of interaction and feedback, the self-regulating processes by which the earth evolves, have been understood for years. For example by engineers such as Tustin and the original exponent of systems thinking, Bertalanffy. Their ideas are widely applied in daily life from power generating equipment to aerospace, video recorders to elevators and biotechnology to economics [2.10, 2.11].

A third is the valuable insight of Arthur Koestler [2.12]. He hypothesises that evolution can be defined in terms of " (a progressive) differentiation of structure and integration of functionality ". This insight bears on complexity since creatures such as apes and human beings clearly operate very effectively as a functional whole. They are also very complex. Observations in the biological world confirm that the high order functionality is accompanied by increased complexity and brain size. Extending this insight, one can hypothesise that, in order to produce great functionality, much attention must be given to identifying the functions and establishing a pattern of relations (integrations and connections) between them which allows them to operate harmoniously as a well-balanced whole.

In relation to the human race I interpret this as follows. Given the rate at which we continue to (over) populate and plunder the planet, fight and deceive ourselves, most of us are unlikely to survive unless we (including the planet) rapidly learn to live and work together more sustainably and globally as one big organism. That is, if we do not evolve in Koestler's sense, we will regress.

In fourth place, though arguably first in order of importance, is Ashby's Law of Requisite Variety, which though not strictly about evolution but derived by Ross Ashby in his work on cybernetics, is very pertinent [2.13]. It may be stated as "the variety in a control system must be equal to or larger than the variety of the perturbations that the entity being controlled is subjected to by its environment, in order to achieve control". In the context of evolution this means that in a niche which exhibits particular environmental conditions, a given availability of resources and certain competing species, a new form or species must have sufficient ability, that is degrees of freedom, to cope with them all if it is going to survive.

This is not the same as being superior in every way in relation to every aspect of the environment and its occupants but does help us identify where some kind of accommodation is necessary. Thus the ability to move rapidly may at once be sufficient to overcome a whole range of potential predator tactics if the predators in the niche are fundamentally ponderous.

In addition, and this requires a stochastic approach to the application of the law, it may be that being eaten is unavoidable from time to time (for some member of a species but not the same member of course!). But, if the numbers of those doing the eating are small and the probability of an encounter very low, then survival may still be possible.

Yet another survival mechanism is the one of interdependency. For example, stickleback fish in a pond may well be eaten by pike. However, if the sticklebacks are the major source of food for the pike, by eating too many sticklebacks the pike will themselves be eliminated. Given a suitably large pond, a steady, continuing state of some pike and some sticklebacks will usually ensue with minor oscillations in the actual numbers over time.

The law of requisite variety is evident all around us. When two football teams play a match the rules of the game are added as a constraint to the physical environment of the pitch, weather, crowd and so on. The constraints are a kind of niche and the two teams compete to score more goals than the other (the "survival" criterion). By dint of recruiting individuals with special foot-balling skills, good management and effective teamwork, a winning team will clearly display more variety than the other and win (survive). A simple example is Forest's very fast left winger outpacing Leeds' defenders and kicking the ball into the Leeds' net at point-blank range.

All games, chess for example, involve the competitors striving to outmanoeuvre the other, that is to achieve a position which the opponent can no longer defend. Each is operating within the rules of the game (niche) to try to create more variety than the other (win / survive).

The same is true of all commercial businesses which compete in many ways within essentially the same legal, environmental and social rules (niche). "Remaining solvent" is the survival criterion.

The fifth person to whom we should refer is Malthus. Where Darwin is famous for his theories of evolution then Malthus is similarly famous for his theory about population. An English economist who died in 1834, Malthus put forward the view that since population increases geometrically and the food supply only arithmetically, then there would come a time when a mismatch would lead to natural occurrences such as famine, disease and high infant mortality. And, if these did not check population growth then war or moral constraint would be needed to do so [2.14].

The theory has been largely dismissed in recent years because it is pessimistic and technology has improved crop yields and food supply. The terms geometric and arithmetic do not hold by strict scientific definition although the general effects might broadly be described as such. Biologists also generally accept that any species has the reproductive potential to multiply until it exceeds the earth's capacity to sustain it. It is simply that in practice the diversity of species, their interdependence and other mechanisms such as predation, keep the sizes of populations in check - Darwin and Gaia theories in action.

It is perhaps timely to reconsider Malthus' hypothesis. During his lifetime food and water were the only obvious constraints on population growth. Today we are not only aware of other constraints, such as the limited ability of the atmosphere to absorb harmful emissions (which still rise in proportion to population) but unsure whether emissions might trigger a cataclysmic change sufficient to reduce the areas of the planet habitable by humans. And Malthus was right about water. There were international conferences in Istanbul and Stockholm, in the Spring of 2009 alone [2.15, 2.16]. They reveal that:

- Children die from water-borne diseases and dirty drinking water at the rate of 5,000 a day
- By 2030 about half the world's population may expect to be living under "water stress", conditions where a shortage of clean water is a serious concern.
- India already has 16% of the Planet's population but only 4% of its water and 3% of its land.

A major implication

What inferences can we draw from the foregoing theories and ideas? It seems our species may not have changed very much physiologically for several thousand years and may not be evolving as individuals at a measurable rate even now. But, the human race is certainly evolving overall as an integral part of the planet (Gaia). The world as it appears to us is very complex and as we should expect of evolution, ever gaining in complexity

(Koestler). It is so complex that mortality rates are incredibly high in the poorest countries and even in parts of the so-called developed world. Individuals cannot respond to the external variety with which they are confronted (Ashby) and they fail to survive as predicted (Darwin). Carbon emissions, shortages of water and an ever increasing global population suggest we are reaching, or may have already over-reached, the practical limits of what the planet can sustain (Malthus).

Popper offers hope. He believes that the human race is capable of solving problems in its search for a better life. Ashby's Law leads to the suggestion that we might add some feature or features, to the attributes of the race as a whole to take into account the increasing variety and changes to our environment we previously failed to address. If we were to do so it is comforting to know that such an increase in complexity would be consistent with what Koestler predicts is a feature of a higher form of life; in this case the "corporate life" of the human race.

But it is possible to go further. I argue in this book that it is the niche in which we strive to survive which holds the key to sustainable progress and survival. Humankind exhibits an amazing range of intellectual skills and abilities and is at least special in this regard. As a result we have developed to such an extent that in common with all others in the industrialised, developed world I do not currently fear starvation, being eaten by a wild animal nor being poisoned by polluted water. Food is not yet a problem and while the prospect of ill-health is a concern, healthcare is available. Even if I die, the net mortality rate for untimely death is minute for UK citizens. I am extremely well serviced and protected and from the perspective of my comfortable home in Nottingham totally unchallenged by the physical environment. That is provided I am credit worthy; in work, or in receipt of a pension or social benefits. Without these I might find myself living off the land, in a cardboard box or worse. But it is unlikely. At least in the industrialised developed world, the free-market, capitalist system has created wealth, sufficient even to provide the most disadvantaged humans with some kind of life support. Humankind has created its own niche and created a generation which is largely insensitive to the planet which surrounds it. **This niche is the capitalist system.**

It is really a niche within a niche, a kind of cage, and as with all cages it protects those inside as well as those without. Unfortunately this cage was devised and developed before we discovered that the resources and behaviour of the wider niche were finite. That wider niche is of course our Planet. Now, free-market capitalism is clearly failing many of the world's population and, in the hands of our leaders and banks, has recently brought the developed world close to a catastrophe which may yet befall us (Chapters 1 and 3). It is becoming difficult to survive in even our adopted niche. Capitalism may be the best idea to date but the signs are it is now unfit for purpose. The cage only protects us while the external conditions, that is the wider niche we call our Planet, do not change and this is no longer the case. It only ever protects some of us anyway (witness Africa's poverty and the underclass in the USA) and is clearly open to abuse from those who have access to the levers of capitalism such as banking and the big corporations. As it stands capitalism requires continuous growth and consumption, neither of which resonate with a sustainable future and the interests of the Planet per se.

Hypothesis

The hypothesis is therefore that we live in a human-forged, dominant niche called capitalism. This niche is obstructing adaptation to, and mitigation of, climate change and our consumption of the finite resources of our Planet. It fails to deal with global poverty and encourages unsustainable human activity and population growth. Humans, especially those in the developed world which consumes most and causes most environmental damage, simply respond to the law of capitalism – be credit worthy or die. Intervention is therefore required to achieve the flexibility and variety of response from individuals within the capitalist niche which Ashby's law suggests is appropriate. Such intervention has to be universal because the problems are global and themselves systemic. Such intervention must affect everyone because it must help to determines the niche we all share. Intervention is about changing our adopted niche so that individuals and the *Big Society* are constrained to be both credit worthy and good citizens of the Planet Earth.

Notes and references for chapter 2

2.1   *In 2008 China's CO_2 emissions exceeded those of the USA, the previous worst polluter. Both produce approximately 6000 million tonnes of CO_2 per year but the per capita value for China is considerably less than that in the USA. Europe's 2006 total was 4,721 million tonnes per year.* NOAA, Mauna Loa Observatory.

2.2   Jackson, M.C., *Creative Holism for Managers,* John Wiley and Sons, England, 2003, ISBN 0-470-84522-8.

2.3   James Gleick, *Chaos: Making a New Science,* Vintage, 1987, ISBN 0-749-386061.

2.4   Masao Mukaidono, *Fuzzy logic for beginners,* World Scientific Publishing Co. Pte., 2001, ISBN-13: 9789810245344.

2.5   Charles Darwin, *On the Origin of Species: The Illustrated Edition,* David Quammen (Editor), Sterling, 2008, ISBN-10: 1402756399.

2.6   William Durham, *Coevolution: Genes, Culture, and Human Diversity,* Stanford University Press, 1992, ISBN-10: 0804721564.

2.7   *Phosphorus is an essential nutrient for all plants and animals. We get our phosphorus through the food we eat, which has been fertilized by mineral or organic phosphorus fertilizers. But where the phosphorus in our food comes from and how sustainable it is in the long term is often not the topic of debate or investigation.*
Modern agricultural systems are dependent on continual inputs of phosphorus fertilizers processed from phosphate rock. Yet phosphate rock, like oil, is a non-renewable resource that takes 10-15 million years to cycle naturally. While all farmers need access to phosphorus, just 5 countries control around 90% of the world's remaining phosphate rock reserves, including China, the US and Morocco (which also controls Western Sahara's reserves). Studies suggest current high-grade reserves will be depleted within 50-100 years. Further, peak production of phosphorus could occur by 2030. While the exact timing might be disputed, it is widely accepted that the quality of phosphate rock

is decreasing and costs increasing. In mid 2008 the price of phosphate rock reached a peak 800% higher than early 2007.

The phosphorus situation has many similarities with oil, yet unlike oil, there is no substitute for phosphorus in food production. Phosphorus cannot be manufactured, though fortunately it can be recovered and reused over and over again.

Global Phosphorous Research Initiative, December 2009

2.8 *"Darwinism is usually regarded as a cruel philosophy: it depicts 'Nature, red in tooth and claw'; that is, a picture in which nature poses a hostile threat to us and to life in general. My view is that this is a prejudiced view of Darwinism, which has been influenced by an ideology which existed before Darwin (Malthus, Tennyson, Spencer) and has almost nothing to do with the actual theoretical content of Darwinism. It is true Darwinism places great emphasis upon what we call 'natural selection'; but this too can be interpreted in quite a different manner. ----------------*

The old, pessimistic and still accepted view is this: the role played by the organisms in adaption is purely passive. They constitute a very heterogeneous population, from which the struggle for existence, the competition, selects those (on the whole) best-adapted individuals by elimination of the others. The selection pressure comes from without.

Great emphasis is usually put on the fact that all evolutionary phenomena, especially the phenomena of adaption, can be explained only by this selection pressure from without. Nothing is thought to come from within except the mutations, the variability (of the gene pool).

My new optimistic interpretation stresses --- the activity of all living creatures. All organisms are fully occupied with problem-solving. Their first problem is survival. But there are countless concrete problems that arise in the most diverse situations. And one of the most important problems is the search for better living conditions: for greater freedom; for a better world."

Karl Popper, *In search of a better world – Lectures and essays from thirty years,* Routledge, 1992, ISBN 0-415-08774-0.

2.9 *James* Lovelock, *Gaia: A New Look at Life on Earth,* Oxford University Press, 2000, ISBN-10: 0192862189, ISBN-13: 978-0192862181.

2.10 Arnold Tustin, *The Mechanism of Economic Systems,* Heinemann; 2nd Edition, 1957, ASIN: B0000CJQWG.

2.11 Ludwig von Bertalanffy, *An Outline of General System Theory, British Journal for the Philosophy of Science, Vol. 1, No. 2, 1950*

2.12 *"The process of evolution may be described as differentiation of structure and integration of function. The more differentiated and specialised the parts, the more elaborate coordination is needed to create a well-balanced whole. The ultimate criterion of the value of a functional whole is the degree of its internal harmony or integratedness, whether the 'functional whole' is a biological species or a civilization or an individual. A whole is defined by the pattern of relations between its parts, not by the sum of its parts; and a civilization in not defined by the sum of its science, technology, art and social organisation, but by the total pattern they form, and the degree of harmonious integration in that pattern."*
Arthur Koestler, *The Sleepwalkers*, Arkana (Penquin), 1959.

2.13 *The Law of Requisite Variety: if a system is to be stable the number of states of its control mechanism must be greater than or equal to the number of states in the system being controlled. Ashby states the Law as "only variety can destroy variety".*
Ashby, W.R., *An Introduction to Cybernetics*, Chapman and Hall, 1956, ISBN 0-416-68300-2.

2.14 Allan Chase, *The Legacy of Malthus,* University of Illinois Press, 1980, ISBN-10: 0252007905, ISBN-13: 978-0252007903.

2.15 Fifth World Water Forum, Istanbul, Turkey, 16 to 22 March, 2009.

2.16 World Water Week, Stockholm, 16 to 22 August, 2009 (annual conference).

Chapter 3:
Capitalism

"Credit is a system whereby a person who cannot afford to pay gets another person who cannot pay to guarantee that he can pay."

Charles Dickens (1812-1870)

How capitalism has evolved and the principal features of the financial services sector. The growth imperative, wealth creation divorced from things of true value and opportunities for unbridled self interest. Market development, the principal ideas which have dominated recent progress. The self-interest of the Planet.

Currency

Systemic change to the capitalist system is a theme of this book. It is only fair therefore to clarify what I mean by capitalism.

In the modern world it is self-evidently difficult to survive unless backed by credit or money and virtually impossible to enjoy life's benefits without them. Even barter, the negotiated exchange of goods, is and always has been, very limited in scope and convenience. What does someone who has nothing, exchange for food and water in the world of today? But as early as 6000-9000 years ago it seems that cattle, sheep, camels, grain and other forms of produce were used as a kind of money. The idea of money clearly had merit, so by 1200 BC mollusk shells had been adopted and the first metal money, initially in a shell-like form, was quick to follow. In China this base-metal money became more rounded with use and led to the first "coinage". Paper money first appears in China around 800 AD.

Outside China at around 500 BC, in Lydia (part of Turkey as we now know it), money was produced from silver, gold and copper and the techniques subsequently copied by the Persian, Greek, Macedonian and

Roman empires. The coins, being of precious metal, possessed inherent value in themselves. The utility of money soon caught on and spread with the movements of people who were familiar with the concept. Roman coins are still discovered in the UK and the spread of money to use as "currency" in facilitating transactions is simply a consequence of conquest and migration.

Whether the coins and notes of a particular currency have inherent value or are merely tokens accepted to be of a given value by all who use them, is an interesting point we rarely consider. A token with the head of the Emperor Hadrian was of base metal and of little inherent worth but so long as everyone accepted it at "face" value it served well as money. Being an Emperor with a sizeable army, Hadrian undoubtedly had little difficulty in ensuring that its value was respected, besides which, it was in the general interest that the consensus held. Provided Hadrian didn't create too much currency, thereby devaluing what had already been issued, and prevented forgers from undermining the entire system, money was a flexible tool for facilitating trade and giving individuals incentives to do whatever the paymasters felt necessary.

Between 1816 and 1930 the USA and UK used tokens which were valued according to how much gold they represented and could thus be traded directly alongside gold of the same quality and weight. Some coins such as gold sovereigns were both a token and a coin of intrinsic value. In 1930, as a result of the great depression, the gold standard was abandoned and today money is generally valued according to the economic strength of the country or countries which issue it and relative to other countries which issue currencies. In extremis some countries issue more currency than their economies justify and the result is inflation, that is a reduction in what a unit of the currency will buy today compared with yesterday, and a lack of credit (and credibility) in the international markets i.e. a currency which lacks credibility (based on a suspect economy) will have a poor exchange rate against a stronger currency (based on a strong economy).

Gold is still valued as a reserve. People rushed to buy Krugerrands in the 1990s because they were made of gold as well as having a value in South African currency, the rand. In 2010 the price of gold is at a very high level; a good investment when the stock markets are still recovering from the 2008 fiasco and currencies are suspect [3.1].

Many transactions are now conducted electronically using computer systems to adjust the change of value in the seller's and buyer's accounts. We thus have a digital form of currency which relies on systems to hold accounts very securely and permit only authorized amendments to them via passwords and encrypted communications. Credit cards and internet banking are familiar examples of using electronic currency. Of course such currency may be exchanged for coins or notes, it is simply more convenient to use for some transactions.

A good introduction to money, capitalism and the 2008 crisis, is Nial Ferguson's book and associated Channel 4 television series, "The Ascent of Money" [3.2].

Mechanism

While money, or more generally the term "currency", has clearly evolved as a means of facilitating the exchange of things of value and allows individuals to store money for future transactions, it is not capitalism per se. Capitalism refers to the systems which have grown up on the back of currency and the ways in which those systems are manipulated by governments and those who have a use for currency; that is pretty well everyone. The principal stages and features in the development of capitalism are as follows.

Stage 1: Supply and demand

Money is used as a token without intrinsic value per se. Individuals obtain money by selling their labour to create products or provide services for "others". Then, as these "others" they use their money to buy the products and services they need. Capitalism is thus characterised as having a **supply side** and a **demand side** as shown in Fig. 3.1(a). It all works very well if the same people provide both the supply-side labour to create products and service and the demand-side consumption and purchasing power to buy what is created. Money circulates continuously from supply-side to demand side to supply-side in one direction and goods, services and labour, circulate in the other.

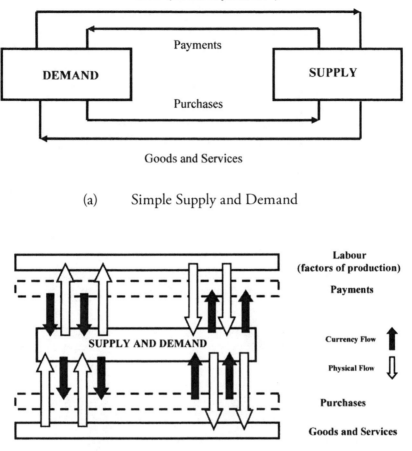

(a)   Simple Supply and Demand

(b) Generalised form of Supply and Demand

Figure 3.1 Supply and Demand

Of course businesses also carry out a lot of business-to-business (B2B) transactions, such as buying in materials, accountancy and many other goods and services. There are many B2B exchanges in the manufacturing supply chains from mining of raw materials to the foundries, rolling mills and engine manufacturers of the automotive and aerospace industries for example. In addition the Government taxes individuals and businesses and it too is really just another supplier of services (public) for payments. It employs people, pays their salaries and delivers what is democratically agreed. It differs only in so much as it is an imposed part of the supply chain from which neither individuals nor businesses can opt out. In general, businesses contribute to both demand and supply as shown in Fig. 3.1(b) as does the Government. The fundamental point remains, that for a sustainable system, the money spent with suppliers **must equal** the money paid by those suppliers to those who spend. The actual timescale over which the equality should achieve balance must be closely related to the time taken by the production and purchasing activities concerned and the need for wages to be paid at sensibly short intervals. The timescale for balance is thus closer to months than decades.

Stage 2: Savings and stocks, deflation and inflation

Provided supply and demand are equal all is therefore well. But on the demand side human beings like to feel secure and set aside some of the money they earn. Imagine a physical store, such as a money box, in which they place such savings. The savings are held to cover contingencies or as a means of purchasing items sometime in the future. The demand side thus takes money out of the system, at least in the short term, and so supply and demand move out of balance. The supply side receives less income and it cannot pay the earlier level of wages to everyone employed. It is forced to press its workers to take lower wages and even to make some redundant. Demand falls and prices follow in an attempt by suppliers to maintain sales. The initial result of savings is deflation.

Similarly companies build up stocks to cover fluctuations in demand and future sales which extracts value from the supply side. However this has an inflationary rather than deflationary effect since there is then more demand than supply, prices can increase because of scarcity of supplies and workers seek higher wages.

Stage 3: Appreciation and depreciation

One might suppose that provided stocks and savings were in themselves of equal value or balanced, inflation and deflation effects would cancel out. Unfortunately the balancing of supply and demand is too complex for this to hold true. For example, when some purchased items such as services, food and entertainment are consumed, the value of the service, food or entertainment is exchanged for money. However, while the money continues to exist the purchased item disappears. Its value has been consumed but the money is available to take part in a further value exchange. Other items such as property, nonetheless continue to have value for possibly hundreds of years and in recent times property has appreciated in value by amounts which are of the same order annually as individuals are paid for full employment. Yet others, such as cars, refrigerators and clothes lose value over time because they cease to function due to wear and tear, they depreciate.

In practice stocks, savings, employment and the value of money achieve a crude ever-changing equilibrium but both savings and stocks represent value which is extracted at current prices for re-injection sometime in the future at what might be totally different prices. Fundamentally, savings on the demand side and the building of stocks on the supply side tend to drive the system out of balance and the monetary value of the out-of-balance changes over time.

The situation is made more complicated still by the inherently dynamic definition of value. The interchange of labour, goods and services represents what is generally called "the market" in which the monetary value of any exchange is determined by the two sides of any transaction. For example, if a week of my labour produces one table and I am paid three pounds for the table, both the table and a week of my labour are valued at three pounds. If I turn to making cabinets and can produce one cabinet each week and get four pounds, my week and the cabinet are both valued at four pounds. Cabinet making is thus worth more than table making at that point in time. Of course when everyone who wishes to have a cabinet owns one the market for cabinets disappears. A cabinet would be worth nothing as would be a week of my time making one.

In practice the supply and demand model of Fig. 3.1 is subject to variations in the monetary value placed on labour, goods and services by the "market". Stocks may or may not be sold in future, at prices which may or may not be higher than those which applied at the time they were laid down. The same holds for the costs of the raw material and labour from which the stocks were made. Some purchased items such as property may change in value significantly. In 2009 house prices rose in the UK by an average of nearly 6% on an average house price in excess of £150,000, that is by more than £9000 and greater than a third of the UK average per capita income.

But currency as defined so far, is simply an intermediary for representing value. The Government issues currency (coins and notes) and, depending on the quantity issued, the complex process of supply and demand across an enormous variety of services, products and employment opportunities determines the price of an item and affordable rates of pay. The Government thence does its best to set out policies to address concerns like promoting businesses, allocating spending to the public sector, maintaining a legally binding framework for taxation and supporting the socially and economically disadvantaged. It takes advice and uses measurements of economic activity and wages along with quantitative models, based largely on the foregoing theory, to do this as well as possible in line with its political ideology.

As the population increases more currency is issued by Government to recognise the presumed growth and to satisfy the need for people to share in what should be at least proportional increases in total wealth. Wealth that is usually expressed as the Gross Domestic Product (GDP) which is, subject to some finer points of economic definition, the total monetary value of the annual supply-side output (or demand-side consumption).

Stage 4: Interest and growth

Services are consumed and goods wear out. I may purchase a haircut and feel it to be very good value but I have to buy another within a few weeks. As a purchaser the value to me is temporary and does not accumulate. The motor car for which I paid £10,000 some years ago is now worth almost nothing. It may have lasted longer than a single hair cut but it too was temporary. The monies I exchanged for the haircuts and the car remain in the "system" but the value they represented has disappeared and is lost to me. So unless more hair is cut and more cars are built there will be a decrease in employment and hence deflation. But usually more hair is cut and more cars produced. We have a potentially sustainable system since a continuous consumption of goods and services is matched by their continuous provision and payment to the people who produce them. Even high-cost items like cars can be purchased because individuals can put savings aside and car dealers can hold stocks for future sales.

So while I am building up my savings to buy a car for example, they are likely to lie around for some time before they are sufficient and actually needed. There is thus an opportunity for the contents of my and other savers' money boxes to be put to work, to be invested meanwhile in setting up new services and suppliers who pay for new workers. But such investments carry risks, so savers are both careful not to invest in poor opportunities and sensible to charge for what they lend. These charges are what we call **interest** and this becomes a feature of the system; the payment to those with money for the use of their money for a certain time.

An important feature of interest is that it is a step removed from any real-world exchange of value such as a payment for services, goods or labour. It represents an income to the demand side of the economy without a corresponding increase in the supply side. Or more strictly, the increase in the supply side is achieved indirectly either by the beneficiary of the interest buying more goods or via investment, that is the development or expansion of businesses on the supply side. Figure 3.2 illustrates what happens. Additional money flows from the demand side to the supply side. That which is invested supplements the input of labour and along with land, and enterprise (entrepreneurial flair) is referred to by economists as "the factors of production". That which is used for purchasing goods and services is an addition to purchasing power. In both cases **growth is a natural consequence** because production capacity has to increase. The corollary is that a system based on interest must itself grow to remain viable.

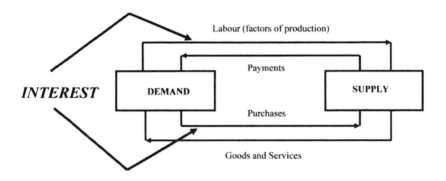

Fig 3.2 Interest and Growth

Stage 5: Banks

As a consequence of stage 4, banks are formed and become a significant feature of the system because they provide useful services such as paying interest on money deposited with them. They are a physically secure repository for money, are a replacement for the money box capable of handling other than just physical currencies and, by holding the money-box savings of many thousands of savers, can assemble huge quantities of money within a single organisation. This latter point is a key feature of capitalism because it enables the banks to invest in projects and businesses which would be beyond the scale of an individual saver. As a single organisation which is investing routinely, it is also worthwhile for banks to employ the specialist skills for assessing the risks associated with those investments. They are also in a position to spread the risks, to invest in many opportunities and through careful management ensure that even if particular investments fail, overall investment succeeds. Savers get the benefits of spreading risk which they could not get individually and often receive a guaranteed rate of interest on their deposits.

Such is the system of high-street banking that savers simply place their money with the bank and receive interest. They are not normally aware of how and where the bank invests its funds. While the funds held by a bank are mostly tied up in investments the banks retain some cash to provide the day-to-day needs of customers. When I decide to spend my savings the bank is able to return (my) money to me with the agreed interest. But, if all customers wanted all their money back at the same time however, the banks would be unable to meet the demand. This is called a run on the bank of which Northern Rock is a recent good example [3.3]. It is impractical for a bank to call in all the investments because the invested money will have already been at least partly spent in creating the longer-term revenues and hence profits with which to pay interest to savers.

Stage 6: Mutual and building societies

Before banking took its current hold on finances, mutual societies were formed by groups of individuals to gain advantage from sharing resources and risks. They offered limited services but essentially allowed individuals to save and borrow within a framework of rules which the group itself set and administered, hence the term mutual. I came across an example in Brazil a few years ago whereby a group of individuals subscribed to a car club. They contracted to subscribe a given amount every month for ten years. Each month the group bought a car and allocated it by lot to one of its members.

In the UK we are familiar with building societies although most have given up their mutuality to become banks (by converting membership into shareholdings in a company which replaced the society). These originally specialised in property or mortgage finance, whereby a customer asks the bank for money to purchase a house under a contract by which the customer pledges to repay the bank from future savings to a sum equal to the price of the house plus interest. The interest to be paid is calculated on the amount of loan outstanding during the period of repayment. Such societies only loaned to members who were expected to deposit savings with the society, possibly for years ahead of being granted a loan (the mortgage).

Mortgage contracts vary, but in essence the bank holds the property as collateral against failure to meet repayments of the loan. If the market price of the property is genuine and the ability of the saver to repay are carefully checked at the outset, the bank will be safely covered by both a repayment contract (over 25 years for example) which will give a defined margin of profit, and by having the property as an asset. This kind of investment is a specific deal between the bank and saver for a particular property.

Stage 7: Retail and commercial banking

There is clearly a difference between lending for the purchase of a house and lending to an individual to set up a business. Houses tend to retain or increase in value and thus provide collateral for the bank (lender) whereas business investment is often a risk since collateral may be weak or difficult to realise should the borrower default. Some banks issue loans only within the limits of their cash deposits. Others lend closer to the value of their investments which are usually much higher but subject to risk.

Broadly, retail or high-street banking refers to straightforward deposits and loans by individuals to enable them to manage their personal finances. This usually extends to mortgages. The customers expect their deposits to be secure both physically and in regard to financial risk. The banks lend only to low risk borrowers and almost always against collateral which, in case of default, can be sold to meet any remaining debt.

Commercial banking refers to investment (stocks and shares) whereby a bank may invest in a business to help it start up or expand. The mechanism may be to buy shares in the business, that is become a part owner with the shares as evidence of the size of shareholding, or simply to lend it money against a contract which charges interest on the loan. Owners of shares do not receive interest but annual dividends. That is, payments derived from the profits of the company and distributed to the shareholders in proportion to their shareholdings. Collateral or security for such investments or loans is less easy to discern than for mortgages (property is substantive) but a business with a good order book simply seeking money to fund the purchase of materials to satisfy those firm orders would be typical of a good investment. Companies entering a new or existing market where the supply side is outstripped by potential demand is another. A new product or transforming technology is more difficult to assess but ventures which may have potentially massive returns are also very attractive. The invention of the steam engine by Boulton and Watt, Stephenson's locomotive and Whittle's jet engine are examples of transforming technologies from which investors and other beneficiaries made fortunes [3.4]. As with mortgages the bank will normally have expertise developed from experience of making many such investments.

Perhaps surprisingly, most companies have continuous overdrafts with banks to pay for stocks and the costs of work in progress. This is because they will normally have to pay their suppliers and employees before they themselves get paid. If the banks ceased to provide credit for these purposes the entire system would collapse. This is what would have occurred in 2008 and 2009 had the banks not been given huge tranches of taxpayers' money to stimulate lending. Many businesses failed nonetheless because loans ceased or proved inadequate.

Stage 8: Stock markets and exchanges

The stock markets or stock exchanges exist because investments have value and may be traded as products in their own right. There is a market for shares and stocks which is carried out in exchanges such as those in London, New York and Tokio. The numbers of shares traded is enormous and the shares of all the world's corporations are traded through them.

Such is the business of trading shares that financial services companies have grown up alongside banks to exploit it, operating on behalf of clients who invest in them to invest in the stock markets. They employ dealers who trade the huge sums of money represented by the shares and other financial products such as hedge funds and derivatives (see below). Bear Stearns, Goldman Sachs and Lehman Brothers are examples, the latter being especially well-known as the first major bankruptcy and catalyst for the 2008 crisis, with losses of $613 billion [3.5].

The average values of shares traded is taken as a proxy for the world's economic health and are quoted in a number of famous indices such as the FTSE (London's Financial Times Stock Exchange), the Nikkei (Japan), Hang Seng (China) and Dow Jones (USA). The role of the stock exchanges is central to the (current) capitalist system. To understand how they operate it is important to appreciate the distinction between (a) the sale of shares to raise funds to implement or run a business (i.e. a means of profiting from an investment in particular business), and (b) the trading of the perceived "market" valuation of shares and other financial products to obtain profit (i.e. a means of profiting from investments which is independent of any one business).

Before it may trade a company must be registered and declare the number of shares into which its owners wish to divide it. The owners may then sell the shares for money which they use to set up and run the business, effectively sharing ownership among shareholders in proportion to the numbers of shares each purchases. There are rules about how this may be done but they are essentially common-sense safeguards to avoid fraud and unfairness. Fundamentally the **initial** sale of shares by a company is a means of raising money (capital) for **sole use** by that company.

However, a person holding shares in one or more companies may offer them for sale to people or organisations which have nothing to do with the companies to which the shares relate. They may moreover sell them for what they can get and such sales or exchanges of shares may be repeated many times. None of this has any direct effect on the company whose shares are being traded. If the price at which its shares are traded in a stock market goes up the shareholders, employees, directors and chief executive are usually pleased since the external valuation of the company appears to be rising. A high price for its shares is a vote of confidence. The company is perceived to have performed well and is likely to continue to do so. But the share price in the stock market does not alter the balance sheet of the company. The balance sheet simply contains the number of shares issued and at the price obtained when they were initially issued. It is also the case that regardless of a company's performance its share price in the stock market may vary, and often does, with current affairs and political decisions both domestic and foreign. If a war is imminent somewhere the share prices of defence companies will rise. A 'flu epidemic or mere threat of one will give shares in drug companies a boost and so on.

Stock-market prices rise and fall so they provide an indication of how the "market" sees a particular company and indirectly has an effect on how customers and the workforce regard it. This may have an indirect effect on its operations but as a general rule, unless there is a major change in a company's share price in the stock market, its day-to-day operations are unaffected. Unless the company issues new shares, there is no income or loss to a company because of stock-market activities. The "wealth" created by the stock markets through trading shares arises from the commissions paid to the traders for managing the share transactions. Since the value of shares transacted is very high these commissions may be very large. They are effectively a charge on the perceived value of a company's shares to the shareholder and ultimately a deduction from the future wealth created, or projected to be created, by the workers in that company.

The difference between the purchase price of a group of shares and the price at which it is later sold will be a gain or a loss to the particular shareholder. Unless the stock market is growing overall, as shown by the relevant index, there is no net profit across all investments due to trading shares (only from dividends on the original shareholdings which are a matter for each company and outside stock-market control). To be a winner, a shareholder has to study the markets and factors which influence them. When a shareholder makes a gain the money comes from the actual or projected increase in performance of the company whose shares were transacted. No new wealth is created per se but the investor takes cash today from a forecast of wealth sometime in future (which may or may not happen depending on future events). When the stock market index is rising the investors will on average be contemplating profits and the extraction of wealth from the system (a bull market). When the indices are falling investors are forecasting prospective losses (a bear market).

Whether investment is in a particular company (as in (a) above) or in the stock market (as in (b)), it is at risk. However, in the first case the investor is a shareholder and entitled to attend shareholders meetings and vote on the appointment of the chief executive and board of directors. The investor can influence the company and its performance and has a vested interest in the company doing well. Ultimately that shareholder is tied to the company's success or failure. Such use of money and shareholdings is regarded as being part of the so-called "real economy".

Even this shareholding mechanism is open to abuse, at least from the company's and its employees' points of view. A company which has a lot of valuable machinery or other saleable assets may have more value in these assets than the total value placed on it by the stock-market's estimation of the worth of its shares. An alert and large investor may deliberately buy a majority of that company's shares to then sell off the assets and make a profit. The company ceases to exist and its workforce are out of work. That may be good for the market and economy by weeding out the unfit companies. It may also destroy whole industries and lose valuable know-how for reasons which are spurious or temporary. The phenomenon is called "asset stripping". High-tech companies have been bought by ruthless individuals because their high level of research and development costs, the very reason they were able to compete, could be slashed and taken as short-term profits before that company's inevitable demise.

In case (b), where shareholders trade shares, the rights as a shareholder are the same as in case (a), but in practice the whole purpose of trading shares and the motivation of the shareholders is the trading itself. The objectives are to ensure profits and high-returns. Short-term profits can be obtained by buying shares which are rising in price and selling them when they are perceived to peak. Those who invested in railway companies in the very early days of steam were thought to be seriously in danger of losing their money, but their fortunes were made when railways later straddled the nation. The railways also reduced costs for the cotton industry and many others for whom transport costs were previously high. Investors in cotton mills were thus rewarded too. Railways took business from the canals because they were quicker and investors in canals needed to be sharp to move their investments elsewhere. The software for personal computers has made fortunes for Microsoft investors and many others too. The trick for an investor is to pick a winner which isn't so obviously a winning idea to everyone else, before the bandwagon rolls and dilutes the uniqueness of that idea. Or, having sufficient money, to invest in something early knowing success is virtually certain though maybe years ahead. Fuel cells are today's case in point [3.6]. They are a highly efficient and clean electricity-generation technology which could be used to power cars, combined heat and power (CHP) units and are well suited to geographically remote and mobile power applications. According to the Carbon Trust, mass market applications of fuel cells could save the UK up to seven million tonnes of CO_2 a year in 2050, equivalent to taking two million of today's cars off the road. However, if it's well known enough to be mentioned here you are already too late!

Banks and others who make a business out of trading shares, appoint fund managers who generally specialise in certain sectors of the markets such as commodities, industrial, medical, food, drink and so on. These fund managers manage the movement of funds on behalf of their clients. Money made through these transactions is often regarded as the "non-real economy". As with hedge-fund operations, those with large sums of money to invest can spread risk across a large number of companies and by studying share movements and knowing that when some markets are up others are as a consequence down, able to virtually guarantee a profit. At worst they can afford to wait until the market rises.

Of course fund managers who hold funds on behalf of banks, the very rich, large corporations and pension schemes, are obviously keen to ensure the value of those funds is maintained and increased. When they move their investments they have a significant influence on the perceived value of the shares they exchange so others follow their lead. Yet others may learn, before they are announced in a company's annual report of its good or bad performance. They may thus sell or buy its shares with some foreknowledge of how such impending news is likely to affect certain share prices. Exploitation of foreknowledge or "insider trading" as it is called, is illegal. It is nonetheless difficult to believe it doesn't occur, the temptations are enormous and it is difficult to detect (see also short selling below). A director who holds a large number of shares in his company who knows it is about to crash can too easily off-load them before the price falls. A financial journalist can too easily write an article to affect a share price and exploit the consequential change in value (3.7). More worrying still are the structural weaknesses which build in opportunities for corruption. As economist, academic and Nobel prize winner, Joseph Stiglitz observed of the US federal banking system in 2010, "The regional reserve banks ... have a key role in regulation and in the last (2008) crisis of bailing out the banks. But the heads of these organisations are chosen by a committee dominated by the big banks that are being bailed out ... so the people bailing out are appointed by the people they bailed out".

Stage 9: Hedge funds

Once huge sums of money are available for use by a single organisation there are numerous ways it can be used profitably. One way is through hedge funds for which the following is a typical example.

A farmer in the West Indies is about to sow a sugar crop for future harvesting, transport, processing and sale in the global retail and industrial markets for sugar. The farmer is concerned about uncertainties from seasonal climate variations to unforeseen problems with the harvest or any of the many activities which must succeed to bring the crop to market at a profit. The hedge-fund manager thus negotiates a price for the crop with the farmer who is willing to sell at a discount in return for the hedge-fund manager taking away his concerns. The hedge-fund manager thence sells on the crop at any time right up to the final sale in the global market. Indeed the same crop may change hands several times in the period between the crop being planted and its final sale. The degree of uncertainty changes as the quality and yield of crop becomes apparent, so its value goes up and down accordingly. Those dealing in hedge funds can decide whether to sell for profit when the perceived value increases, or to sell to minimise loss should the perceived value fall. The idea and processes involved are very simple.

The route to profit is however more intriguing. In a particular year, crops in the West Indies may be of poor or good quality, low or high yield, who knows? A hedge-fund manager will thus try to buy crops around the globe to reduce risk, to ensure that after regional variations in actual harvests he still makes a profit. He also knows that the value of sugar will rise if a shortage occurs because food products and companies require sugar for their own products and survival. The market for sugar products and their value will automatically adjust to the availability and demand for sugar. If a hedge-fund manager is able to buy sufficient sugar at the crop stage it is then well placed to manipulate the market to ensure a profit. The scale of such financial investment is itself a hedge against making a loss and reduces risk. For example, in July 2010, Armajaro, a commodities hedge fund, took delivery of 240,000 tonnes of cocoa beans which represented nearly all of Europe's cocoa inventory and enough to make five billion chocolate bars.

Stage 10: Short selling

Short selling is illegal in some countries but not in the UK. It refers to the practice whereby a fund manager, in this case referred to as a dealer or trader, may borrow shares from some other fund manager and give them back at a later date. As long as the number of shares borrowed and paid back is the same, the lender is not unduly bothered because his shareholding doesn't change. The borrower meanwhile sells the shares because he believes the market for those shares is set to fall and the price of the shares with it. If this prediction is borne out, the borrower buys back the number of shares he sold at the now lower value. He repays the lender in shares (not value) and hence makes a profit. The process may take only a few days, hours even. You may think the lender is somewhat naive, but of course he may be paid a commission on the deal and be doing the same thing with other shares in a quasi-reciprocal arrangement with other traders. It is in his interest to collaborate. Of course the whole process is a gamble and the shares could go up not down. But knowledge of the markets favours the borrower and if, after borrowing the shares, the borrower anonymously starts a false rumour that the shares are likely to fall because of some problem with the company's products or profitability, the market will duly respond with the desired fall in its share price. Subsequently, and after the return of shares, the share price assumes its true market value and it seems no harm has been done. But, the profit or loss from short selling is the dealers' not the shareholders'. The money obtained is actually a charge on the future value of the shares used in the short-selling transaction. No new wealth has been created although some individual traders are richer. I leave it to the reader to decide whether gaining or losing such huge sums of money by the use of the money of third parties (shareholders funds) in this way, is either ethically or economically sound?

Personally I see no exchange of value whatsoever but simply an extraction or injection of a large amount of money, which has considerable value in the wider world, for no product or service at all. The concept of money having no intrinsic value except as a token of exchanging items of equivalent value is totally absent. The meaning of value is destroyed. The "system" provides a means of creating cash for use today from a somewhat ephemeral estimate of the wealth others may, or may not produce sometime in the future. If the net flow of such artificial value in and out of the real world were zero, balanced by equal gains and losses, one might not quibble. Unfortunately when there are gains they are for the dealers and banks. When catastrophe descends it is the taxpayer who meets the shortfall. In between catastrophe and success the balance of probability favours the dealers and banks. Enormous profits and bonuses year-on-year provide evidence that this is the case. The markets are in any case largely understood and open to possible manipulation by the very people who trade in them.

In November 2010, the FBI raided the offices of two hedge funds in pursuit of insider trading which is illegal. The raid was part of an initiative by the US Attourney's Office and the US Securities and Exchange Commission (Wall Street Regulator) to clamp down on insider trading and more generally get a grip on so called "expert networks". These have expanded during the first decade of the millennium from around three to 40 in number. Their line of business is to seek out information from players in the real economy, executives and gatekeepers in key corporations, which might foretell a movement in the value of certain corporate shares. They sell the information to investors who may then be unfairly well placed to make big profits very quickly by moving their funds ahead of changes in share price which to them alone are predictable. The problem for the regulators is determining what is insider information and what is not, what can be proved and what cannot.

Stage 11: Derivatives

Derivatives is a term used to describe a wide variety of so-called financial products or packages which can be traded. The financial-services sector has been very creative for more than a decade, in the US and UK particularly, in developing these "products". Mortgages, insurance policies, business investments and hedge funds may all be regarded as assets because future revenue is expected from them. They may thus be used as collateral in raising loans or more frequently sold to purchasers who wish to put their money to work and gain interest (future revenues). Derivatives are simply a way of putting combinations of these assets together with simple descriptions, a tidying- up or gift-wrapping process of various combinations of high- and low-risk investments. There is a large market for such products because the global savings of individuals and profits of businesses are, with the odd exception being held in a box under some bed, all available for investment.

The Chinese are avid savers and the surge in economic activity in China has resulted in huge sums of money seeking good investments. Unfortunately it is hard to find sufficient numbers of good investment opportunities for all the savings available. The effect of large quantities of savings with no place to invest means no income to provide interest which can be paid to savers and interest rates fall. There has thus been great pressure in the past two decades to seek and invest where risks were previously considered too high.

Stage 12: Collateralised Debt Obligations and Credit Default Swaps

Once banks began to have more savings and funds than they could invest in low-risk products they naturally invested in riskier products in order to obtain income with which to pay interest. They then needed to develop ways of reducing these risks; to reduce their exposure to potential debt should any investments fail. This is why Collateralised Debt Obligations (CDOs) originated. CDOs reduce the amount of debt, and hence risk, on a bank's balance sheet.

For example, a bank may have some mortgage loans which are worth £100,000. This bank may then sell a CDO based on these loans to another bank. The second bank thus has what is called a bond (contract) backed by the mortgage loan. Therefore, as the mortgage is paid back, the second bank receives the mortgage interest payments.

However, if people default on their mortgages, then the person owning the CDO is going to see a decline in the value of the CDO. The first bank has in effect sold on its mortgage loans to another company. So, if the person with a mortgage defaults, the risk is born by the person who bought the CDO. The first bank may have lost the mortgage repayments but has pocketed payment for the bond and eliminated exposure to the risk.

The Credit Default Swap (CDS) is a similar concoction to the CDO which applies to any traded financial product whether from a bank, government or a finance house. The buyer of a CDS pays a premium for effectively insuring against default on a debt and receives a lump sum payment if the default occurs. If the debt continues the seller of the CDS receives monthly payments from the buyer [3.8].

CDOs and CDSs are in one sense insurance policies – payments for covering the loss, that is failure of an investment. In another sense they may be used (abused maybe a more appropriate word) when they are used essentially to gamble.

The CDS is especially versatile for gambling purposes since it allows a dealer to buy a CDS from a hedge fund based on the projected movements in value of some (financial) product. For example, assume a deal is based on the CDS owner paying up when the value of a financial product FP1 falls in value by more than 5% from an initially agreed price. If FP1 doesn't fall then the buyer continues to pay the premium to the hedge fund. If the value does fall by more than 5% then the CDS owner pays. Amazingly, neither the hedge fund nor the dealer need have any connection or ownership of FP1. This is not just gambling but gambling with a bias in favour of the gambler because he also has keys to the casino. (I find myself increasingly ashamed of my country which, through its government puts high value on such morally questionable activities.)

Stage 13: State banks

Not strictly a stage but a necessary component of the system is the state bank, the Bank of England for example. This exists because the Government owns the currency system, the minting of coins, printing of notes and authorising of credit. It does not trade at the citizen level but deals with the banks which were set up for the reasons above. The state bank is the agent for injecting or extracting money from that circulating in the exchange between supply and demand. It is normally adjusted in line with Government's wishes. If the Government wishes to issue more money it simply issues bonds which the state bank can sell. State-guaranteed bonds are effectively the printing of money. They have no value other than that which the existing market puts on them. The state bank also sets the interest rates at which banks lend and borrow money. These in turn influence the rates individual savers and borrowers are likely to get or pay at high-street banks. Issuing bonds and setting interest rates are powerful tools by which the state bank and Government can (crudely) influence the way in which the economy performs.

Control

Explanation of the above mechanisms is not especially simplified. It illustrates the principal elements of the capitalist system and their relationships and is relatively easy to understand. What it does not convey, and what is much more complex, is how those relationships work out in practice, what quantities of money, savings, stocks, employment levels and investments are involved and how they vary over time. The answers are, of course, the stuff of economics which is not a particularly precise subject anyway.

There are genuine difficulties because the demand side is constantly changing its needs and the supply side its products and services. Supply and demand are dynamic not fixed and consequently the amount of money in circulation and the propensity, or even opportunity, to save and invest varies continuously. An intervention now may have a tremendous and unexpected effect years later. If savings are high when opportunities for investment are low for example, interest payments on savings can only be met by reducing rates of interest. This in turn discourages saving and money remains in circulation as spending, which improves demand which calls for more investment which thence makes a demand on savings which allows interest rates to rise again and so on – all over a period of time.

The interactions are complex and it is easy to rush to simplistic conclusions when an holistic view is more appropriate (invariably). For example, in 2009 the UK trade deficit was £31bn, the difference between exports of £387bn and imports of £418bn. The financial services sector which includes the banks contributed nearly £42bn to exports and the rest of us contributed £345bn. The financial press quickly claimed credit for the value of the financial sector to the UK economy, making up nearly half the trading deficit for goods. But is this as good as it seems?

First, the Brazilian, Russian, Indian and Chinese (BRIC) economies have huge, untapped markets and investment opportunities for local businesses, based on well-proven products and services from developed countries. Investing in BRIC countries by UK banks is less risky than investing in innovative, entrepreneur-led businesses in the UK, which explains why a large proportion of UK bank profits are obtained from investments abroad. These investments actually increase competition for our exports, especially goods. Export success for UK banks is a measure of impending damage to UK business and UK exports, encouraging foreign competition to develop products to substitute those manufactured here and reducing UK export markets. It is perhaps no coincidence that in November 2010, the UK was annually exporting more to Ireland, a country of around four million people, than it does in combination to the BRIC countries which have a total population of approaching three billion; nearly a half of the global total. If the UK exported a similar per capita amount to the BRIC countries as it does to Ireland, that is by a factor of more than 700, it would cover its national debt several times over within a year.

Second, UK trade statistics have historically separated services and goods, but the distinction is increasingly misleading. Engineering, for example, is also a part of the information economy and provides high-value services as well as "goods". It may be amusing for one sector to claim it alone offsets a deficit but all sectors could make that claim. There is no deficit to which any one sector separately contributes.

Third, financial services depend on the real economy of goods and services to make their profits. They follow the real economy, not vice versa. The majority of us work in the UK's real economy. If the banks increasingly follow the real economies outside the UK the prospects for continuing UK prosperity are dire. There is an ethical point too. We provide much of the working capital for the banks through our savings, interest on business debts and mortgages and large government (i.e. taxpayer-funded) loans. To whom therefore does the financial services sector really owe its success?

In an advanced technological-economy, many investment decisions need to be made years ahead of obtaining a return on that investment because high-tech complex products take many years to develop and bring to market. Governments are thus very concerned about forecasting how the economy will perform in future and how best to influence or even control it. For example, I am concerned that my savings for my retirement will buy something akin to the same value as when I committed the money to savings. If not, then at least any interest earned by those savings should hopefully compensate for any fall in their value. Faith rather than certainty comforts me.

Influence and control of a large beast such as an economy has thus exercised economists and governments since the beginnings of government. In the annals of economic theory Adam Smith, John Maynard Keynes, Milton Friedman and Karl Marx stand above the rest as having had the greatest influence. In truth there are many competing theories and views on what objectives the economic system should serve.

As an engineer rather than an economist, I can readily appreciate that the mechanism described above can be manipulated in many ways towards whatever end the manipulator wishes, normally a government or dictator. However, I can also discern as an engineer that such a mechanism is a multi-variable, non-linear system. Modelling such systems is fraught with difficulty because putting values on the variables is very difficult and because many relationships are non-linear, especially the capricious human element. Even if we had an agreed economic purpose, a consensus on economic theory and were we able to model the system mathematically with confidence, all the uncertainties of chaos theory would apply (see Chapter 6). The intention of any manipulation may thus be clear but, as history demonstrates, whether or not the system will respond to a particular intervention as a particular theory predicts, is highly questionable. One might reasonably question the certainty which prevails among economic experts when science, a much more structured body of knowledge based on testable hypotheses, admits of uncertainty. No wonder economics is sometimes referred to as the dismal science.

Governments are thus forever trying to discern such things as how much money to allow in circulation (the money supply), the interest rates their state bank should charge, the rates of tax and what to tax, what to subsidise if anything and the extent to which it should provide social benefits. What we are witnessing appears to be something governments are loathe to admit, that they are increasingly subordinate to those who run the banks, financial services and the monetary system. Democracy is being undermined and our lives are defined by the rules of capitalism.

In 1776 Adam Smith wrote a treatise of more than 900 pages called "An Inquiry into the Nature and Causes of the Wealth of Nations" and this is considered by many to have changed the world [3.9, 3.10]. Despite the size of this book just three basic principles underpin his ideas and modern capitalism. They are the acceptance of **self interest** as the principal motivation and driver of humankind, the utility of the **division of labour** and the importance of **free markets**. It is the free markets which promote most of the controversy but for past 25 years the free-market form of capitalism has tended to dominate. This is the belief that provided there is competition for goods and services (perfect competition) prices will fall to a minimum, thus meeting the self-interest of the consumer. Thence in search of viable markets some suppliers, also pursuing self interest, will venture into new markets where they have identified new consumer needs. The free market will thus maximise the use of resources and maximise consumer satisfaction.

Adam Smith is also variously quoted by both right-wing and left-wing politicians in support of their world view of how the economy should operate and be "controlled". But he was almost certainly trying to be politically detached and objective. He was not just an economist and his writings range across psychology, ethics, finance, social science and industrial economics. He was not insensitive to the problem of monopolies and was against them. While he felt free markets were generally to be encouraged, some regulation and tinkering by governments was always going to be needed to limit the worst excesses that arise when major corporations dominate a market segment or collaborate in price fixing.

Monetarists, of which Milton Friedman is the best known, are generally in favour of letting markets decide how the economy performs [3.11]. They often quote Adam Smith. Their principal tenet is advocacy of state intervention to control the money supply, that is the quantity of money in whatever form (coin, paper or electronic), circulating between supply and demand. Otherwise they are broadly against governments intervening particularly in the supply side and prefer incentives to taxation as a means of influencing the economy.

Keynesians, named after John Maynard Keynes, a Cambridge University don and economist, believe in more government intervention through setting rates of interest and taxation [3.12]. They believe in fiscal policies which directly affect supply and demand. The proposition that governments should spend money they don't have to stimulate the economy in pursuit of the general good is attributed to Keynes; for example giving the unemployed money. This latter notion was anathema to politicians and economists before Keynes but when there is mass unemployment it has been shown to create demand which begets production which begets trade and hence some degree of prosperity. In the modern, highly integrated global economy it is undoubtedly a government tool but only one among many.

There was also Karl Marx who preached that the factors of production should be owned by the workers. He argued that capitalism, like previous socioeconomic systems, would inevitably produce internal tensions which would lead to its destruction. Just as capitalism replaced feudalism, he believed socialism would, in its turn, replace capitalism, and lead to a stateless, classless society called pure communism. His famous work Das Kapital, was in three volumes, although only the first was published in his lifetime [3.13]. Stalin's USSR put his interpretation of Marx into practice; a planned, supply-led economic model by which production of all the products and services needed by society and the state would be quantified (by the state on behalf of workers) and thence delivered. Production capacity would be exactly matched to demand. Investment and the costs of labour would be calculated as part of the plan. Stocks and shares would not arise since the state owned everything.

Capitalism was thus attacked by communists in the 20th century for what appear in hindsight to have been primarily misconceived, socio-political, power-motivated reasons. The Soviet alternative of a planned, supply-led economy did not succeed and lasted barely 60 years. It didn't work largely because there was little incentive for factories (both the managers and workers) to meet their output targets and there were shortages of almost everything; disastrous for any complex product such as an aircraft, motor car or refrigerator for which the supply chain is long and the number of components large. If what an individual or company is permitted to do is constrained by a plan determined outside their control or influence they can envisage no way to improve their lot or gain satisfaction. They atrophy. Fundamentally, communism failed because it did not realise the value individuals assigned to personal motivation and the opportunity to better one's life. It ignored capitalism's universality and disregarded its ability to semi-automatically stimulate the bottom-up, economic developments which we call enterprise.

So the capitalist, market-led option we currently accept is not perfect and a more constructive and useful approach would be to modify rather than destroy it. The reasons for investigating such modification are now more justified because of the need to address climate change and avoid a repetition of the 2008 financial crisis. Reasons are more credible and objectively defined as this book illustrates. They do not derive from social engineering nor from competition for political power. They point to a need for some form of systemic change which will ensure that, when people behave as Adam Smith perspicaciously explained, each of their countless individual transactions not only serve self-interest but also the interests of the human race and the Planet.

Factors of production and the Planet

So where does the interest of the Planet figure in capitalism? Capitalism as illustrated in Fig. 3.1 contains an obvious weakness. Labour is not the only input to those who supply goods and services. Textbooks on economics more accurately refer to this input as "factors of production" which are defined as the resources required for the production of goods and services; more specifically, land, labour, enterprise and capital. Labour is actually only one component in Fig. 3.1 but we have also mentioned and accepted that capital, in the form of investment, is needed to create the supply side; to kick start the system and provide for growth. It is also self-evident that we need enterprise, that human characteristic which motivates business leaders and entrepreneurs.

But what we have yet to consider is the "land" and it deserves special attention. The land is of course really Mother Earth, the Planet. While it is so easily taken for granted as a readily available resource, **the central theme of this book is to question that very assumption**. Land is not actually ours to give and if we were to be precise about the factors of production we should include the sea, air, fauna, and all the other bounty of the Planet. The Planet is not ours to give. Why should the interest of the Planet be so ignored by the capitalist system? We should question for example the current assumption that countries surrounding the Arctic have ownership of the oil recently found beneath the ice cap and the sole right to exploit it [3.14] ?

Self interest

Adam Smith recognised the need to include human behaviour in any consideration of how economic systems operate. He saw that the multiplicity of exchanges of value, or more correctly perceived value, which make up the economic system, depend on decisions by human beings. Humans are influenced by feelings and motives and self interest is considered to be top of the list (survival is another way of putting it). Self interest is therefore not a trivial parameter in economic modelling.

Adam Smith also reasoned that free markets would operate in a way which, based on the self interest of human beings, reach a stable though slowly changing equilibrium. His ideas and reasoning assume perfect competition and that, out of self interest, no supplier would wish to so overcharge his customers that they cease to buy anything at all. And, no worker would demand such high wages that their employer would cease to employ them.

The concept of perfect competition and the concept of enlightened self interest were always considered to be simplifications but at least sufficiently insightful and useful to use as a basis for economic and political models. While this may have been sufficiently true and helpful in Smith's time it has progressively become less true and even misleading.

The relatively simple economy known to Adam Smith was driven by a work force divided into craftsmen, labourers, seamen, farmers, landowners and merchants. Craftsmen were among the few truly skilled workers against a backdrop of a largely agrarian economy and slow economic and social change, their skills could be passed on to a further generation in the certain knowledge that they would be needed. Merchants and the rich ran essentially family businesses which similarly passed their skills from one generation to the next as almost a god-given expectation. The concept of, and need for new skills and re-skilling, simply didn't arise.

Since the industrial revolution all has changed. It takes around 20 years to educate and train a professional scientist or engineer and around 16 for a good technician. These are very long periods in relation to the rates at which technology and social needs are changing. Decisions by young people to specialise and pursue a particular career are inevitably made many years ahead of entering that career and becoming a true contributor and beneficiary. If through competition the market changes, it is extremely difficult for the individual to adapt and earn the same rewards in a different market. So why should talented young people enter the science and engineering professions which involve a tremendous commitment and effort. It is much easier to opt for accountancy, law, banking and business management. These tend to be generic and transferable skills and can more easily adapt to change.

The market (in the broadest sense) may eventually redress the imbalance when there are no creative people, such as scientists and engineers, and all technology must be imported or foregone. Then, when businesses have nothing they can sell despite their management skills, and lawyers and accountants have lost all their clients, and the banks have nowhere to invest, then skills to produce infrastructure, products and services will once again emerge to be important and valued. The market is a poor and too slow a regulator from this perspective. A control engineer would express the problem as "a difficulty in identifying and thus measuring, the parameters which indicate the direction and nature of change". The consequence is that feedback paths are weak or too slow for effective decisions and control. Responses to change may take a whole generation to have any effect and much talent is misdirected or wasted meanwhile.

Self interest is supposed to prevent a business biting the hand that feeds it by charging so much that it destroys its own markets. However, in the financial services and banking sector the business is centred around individual traders not, as in the engineering and science sectors, by teams of inter-dependent employees whose skills are worth little without the contributions of their colleagues and the often large investments in expensive software, computers, tools and equipment they need.

Even the chief engineer of Rolls Royce (aerospace), valuable and relatively well paid though he is by all but banking standards, requires the entire plant and workforce at Derby and beyond to realise his potential. His self interest is both constrained and augmented by the wider team. The timescale over which his technical decisions must remain valid to ensure a return on investment is often huge – one undetected fault, one crash and a whole generation of aircraft is destroyed [3.15]. For the financial-services trader there are no such constraints; deals are completed within hours and the individual is not constrained by his/her colleagues and knows that banking contributes to infrastructure the taxpayer dare not abandon. If that wasn't apparent before the tax-payers' bail out of the banks in 2008, it is now. Competition and accountability in the real-world market place for the former, and the unreal, speculative world of the latter, are thus totally different. The trader competes on his own with a duty largely to himself; the other is limited by the skills of the team which shares its achievements.

The banking sector is also international. It is able to make huge profits by investing in the enormous local markets of the BRIC countries where the demand for well-proven products and services carry low risks and high returns. This is so much easier than investing in the innovative, high-tech, high-risk ideas of entrepreneurs in the UK.

In addition, while financial services facilitate business development and through insurance-type products reduce risk for many companies who create wealth and together provide the majority with employment, they are actually a cost to those wealth producing companies.

The profits of banks and bonuses of traders are ultimately a charge on the wealth creating activities of the economy as a whole. If the banks had smaller profits and paid smaller bonuses they could afford to charge less for their services. The actual wealth creators, such as the sugar-crop farmer and the industries in which our savings are invested, would then pay less and be able to either reduce their prices, pay their employees more or increase their profits. Tax would be payable on the latter in the same way as tax is levied on bankers. While tax from bankers might fall, the loss to the Government would be totally compensated by a combination of tax from profits in the real economy and a wider distribution of wealth from dividends, wages and lower prices. It is hard not to conclude that the excesses of the financial-services sector are parasitic and distort the fair distribution of wealth.

The emergence of a large public sector which spends a considerable amount of taxpayers' money on health, education, defence, infrastructure and administration is a significant change from the time of Adam Smith. It also distorts the market and, as already mentioned in Chapter 1, the average income of public-sector employees now exceeds that of the private sector; its provision for pensions far outstrips that of the latter. UK public-sector wages and salaries are agreed by negotiation rather than competition and all within an "industry" which cannot "go bust". It is not that a public sector is inherently wrong, it is simply that it is insulated from direct competition and grossly inefficient [3.16, 3.17].

Maybe the foregoing is just a lesson in the unfair nature of life which the losers must learn to accept? Alan Greenspan who was chairman of the US Federal Reserve Board from 1987 to 2006, seems to think it's all down to human nature [3.18]. Mervyn King, Governor of the Bank of England, has a similar view [3.19]. Well one can't argue that human nature hasn't got a capricious and shameful side but morality, good governance and the common law are normally able to constrain it. Maybe there a defeatist element in the content of what these two say or perhaps it's just a cunning attempt on their part, as major stakeholders, to maintain the status quo? Both seem reconciled to history repeating itself. I have news for them. In the 19th century the lessons from history were that man could never fly.

Since then some men have been to the moon and millions now travel by air.

Personally, and in view of the above explanation of how the financial markets operate, I believe there is something fundamentally immoral in the mechanisms by which the markets operate. As an engineer I see this as just another problem to solve.

It is also something we should expect Government to address because over several hundred years our democratically elected governments have gradually reduced the exploitation of one section of society by another. The process has been slow and sometimes painful but in the UK it has eliminated social conflict of the blood-letting kind and improved the standard of living of the most impoverished. Every UK citizen has access to clean water and sufficient food. A minority have poor accommodation but not on the scale and nothing as bad as in Victorian times. Healthcare and education are universal and the average life expectancy continues to rise [3.20]. The quality of life for many is still poor but significantly better than that in the starving communities, disease-ridden slums and child-labour-driven industries of the 18th and 19th centuries [3.21]. Who in the UK today who wants a television set, doesn't own or have access to one?

But is it fair that a 5% annual rise in the value of a £1 million house (£50, 000) is more than twice the earned income of the average citizen? Or that a general practitioner (GP), who as a public servant has no effective competition for his job, should in some cases receive from the public purse, twice the salary of a chartered engineer of comparable if not higher intellectual and practical ability, who creates wealth, pays taxes and fights international competition to do so? Is it fair that the bankers queue to recruit the best graduates in engineering and science and ensure they get the cream by paying high salaries and offering enormous bonuses, not because they are justified nor because the skills required are unique, but because they have the money to do so. Is it fair that this practice denies the rest of us the benefits of these individuals' skills for creating wealth rather than merely manipulating it? Is it fair that a failed chief executive should receive severance payments worth hundreds of thousands of pounds [3.22, 3.23] when many of those for whom he was responsible are made redundant for just a few [3.24] ?

We can surely do better. The majority of people, even students, are never formally introduced to a single work of philosophy. If they were they might take note of John Stuart Mill who believed the only way to measure the morality of an action is to ask if it increases the overall happiness of human beings and minimises their suffering [3.25]. They might question whether capitalism, for all its merits, might not be improved upon. Is there not some way forward which, as its main objective, would embrace the concept of happiness and take more account of those stakeholders who happen not to be corporate shareholders; that is most of humanity and the Planet itself? None of which is inconsistent with the writings of Adam Smith or Karl Popper. It's simply a pity that Adam Smith didn't recognise the Planet in his scrutiny of self interest.

Progress and evolution

So given the current demonstration of how greed and weaknesses in the free-market have taken us, where are we going? It is impossible to predict the future of the human condition and current progress may lead to extinction. Is more of the capitalism which has served us so well until now therefore a sound basis for evolutionary progress? It is clearly questionable from the evidence presented here. So is there an alternative and how in a globalised world, would alternatives co-exist? Communism and capitalism co-existed for several decades so a split is not impossible but two kinds of capitalist systems on a planet with a universal problem, probably not? We have a largely unified capitalist system at present so it is almost certainly easier to modify this than to create something entirely new. Assuming something totally new were in the offing, which it isn't.

In any case, modification is necessary for all the reasons set out in this book. Uncontained competition, continuously competing to get something the other fellow (or nation) might otherwise have, is also dangerous from a global perspective. Competition and growth drive consumption and accelerate the rate at which we deplete the Planet's resources. Productivity improves competitiveness but without growth increases net unemployment and poverty. It also puts pressure on incomes and encourages individuals to work hard for long hours. To sustain the system consumption in turn becomes a driver of this vicious cycle – growth through consumption. Families are unintentionally neglected because both parents need to work to pay for what they perceive they need. The working week in the UK is the longest in Europe and it now requires two average incomes to be able to purchase a modest house or flat. This forced pre-occupation with work weakens society because individuals are too busy to participate in community affairs.

Could we not share the work and benefits more effectively? Do we need so much work and consumption in the first place? Of course not, it is a consequence of the capitalist system and a condition of survival in the artificially-created, capitalist niche. Drawing on their recent studies of population growth, Christensen and others conclude that the 21ˢᵗ century will be about the re-distribution of work in a similar way to the 20ᵗʰ having been about the re-distribution of wealth [3.26]. It is an inspired insight which is as relevant at the level of states as it is for individual people. It fits with the idea of the *Big Society*.

Whatever we do, capitalism and population growth as they are now, fuel growth and consumption, the enemies of global sustainability.

Competition

A hundred years ago the tradition was to supply goods predominantly from locally sourced items, sold through locally owned companies specialising in one type of product. Today the dominant tradition is that we have globally sourced goods distributed and sold via trans-national corporations by way of massive supermarkets offering a wide range of products. From the consumers point of view seasonal food variations are hardly perceptible and many products are defined by the brand of the supermarket rather than that of the originator. Supermarket brands are becoming better known than the original producers' and the supermarkets thereby control access to large sections of the food market. Nevertheless, there are residues of the earlier traditions and such businesses as nurseries, local tradesmen and some small shops remain. Local farmers supply niche markets for organically grown crops, whole carcasses of meat and so on. In fact most of the traditional methods of retailing still exist in a minor way alongside the new which include internet ordering and home deliveries.

To compete in these markets is very tough. You either need a unique product or service no-one else can provide (a monopoly) or you need to seriously compete. Traditionally competitiveness was achieved by demonstrating advantage in some aspect of your product or service – better quality, lower price or excellent customer service. In the past 30 years, under pressure from highly productive manufacturers, especially in the early days from Japan and Taiwan, it has become necessary to be competitive in all three aspects. This is partly due to increased competition in the market place but also due to world-wide improvements in methods of manufacturing and delivering services.

Total quality management (TQM) which was conceived and developed in Japan by (ironically) the American W. E. Deming, revolutionised how quality should be approached. The old way was 100% checking of the final product; a not particularly foolproof method anyway. TQM is a philosophy by which such things as "right first time" and "empowerment" give the person on the job the responsibility and authority needed to do it well. If a process or component is potentially faulty then detect it before allowing it to proceed, before putting more work into it and adding costs which can never be recovered [3.27].

Just in time (JIT) methods contributed too. Don't store up inventory in vast amount of work in progress. Don't make something until you need it. Reduce batch sizes, stocks and material handling, simplify sequences of production and eliminate bottlenecks [3.28].

More recently still came the identification of the value chain by Michael Porter which seeks to identify where in a manufacturing or service organisation value is added and perhaps more importantly where it is not; the latter being a target for elimination [3.29]. It was complemented by Business Process Re-engineering (BPR), which like TQM and JIT can be applied to service industries and the public sector [3.30, 3.31]. BPR aims to break down barriers between organisational functions so that product and service delivery became more efficient and streamlined. It is well supported by methods and tools for mapping product and information flows and how tasks and responsibilities are linked together. The tools reveal weaknesses and hence ways to improve.

To all the above may be added the concept of lean manufacturing [3.32], much beloved by the automotive industries, and continuous improvement or Kaizen, which acknowledges its Japanese origin. Kaizen refers to the policy of continuously seeking to improve [3.33].

So we all know quite a lot about how to compete and remain slaves to the free market.

Markets

Because of international competition there is therefore constant change and evolution in the sourcing, distribution and sale of goods with a concomitant need for effective and efficient management in both the public and private sectors. Advantage can clearly be gained by successfully predicting future change and hence being in position to exploit it. Unfortunately prediction is a tricky business and even computers and communications technology (ICT) and the almost limitless gathering of data are unable to deliver a crystal ball. However, a recent book by Zuboff and Maxmin supplies an intriguing view about what is likely to happen and is beginning to happen already [3.34].

They have developed the concept of the "support economy". This is based on the striking observation backed by evidence, that corporations are progressively failing to service their markets. That is to say they are failing US in meeting OUR needs. They cite several thousand references in a scholarly tome which concludes that we need to change and are about to enter a new episode in the development of capitalism.

In brief, they point out that ownership and control of capital and factors of production continue to evolve. The single embodiment of both ownership and control in the lord-of-the-manor-type, owner-manager structures of the distant past, by which the majority of the population had little choice but to accept what was on offer in terms of work and subsistence let alone play, have been largely replaced by shareholding companies. These companies, mostly big corporations, define the current tradition whereby ownership is invested in shareholders and control is separated from it through its delegation to management teams. This Zuboff and Maxmin describe as **managerial capitalism** and argue very credibly that it is failing. In its place they see emerging what they call **distributed capitalism**. In this, considerable control passes to us as individuals and citizens. Instead of being regarded by those who sell us goods as a customer whose needs are defined by corporate executives, we become individuals who define ourselves and our own needs. These needs are then met by organisations, often working in federation with others, which supply a whole range of services based on those needs and extending effectively into our personal lifestyles. These would cover many domestic chores such as handling insurance, holiday arrangements, investments, house maintenance, hobbies, childcare, schooling and so on. Mostly a much more intimate and personalised arrangement which frees us to live the lives we wish to lead as individuals and families.

A factor in this development is the staggeringly fast and effective developments in ICT. A support economy is impractical without it. Only through the use of technology can the flexibility and responsiveness required be achieved effectively (manufacture and distribution are also required and need technology which is sustainable too). This kind of economy is what Zuboff and Maxmin call systemic, more to do with changes of structure and relationships than it is with revolution in a destructive sense. Companies will still make products and supply services but they will do so on the basis that the adding of value by whatever they do extends into the processes which were hitherto left to individual customers. For example, instead of a company selling house insurance as a package to you, it will for a fee undertake to ensure you are well looked after in the event of any kind of mishap. Value is added not merely by selling financial packages as now, but by understanding lifestyles and on doing what is really required, namely providing convenience, security and comfort. Value is added and obtained through a relationship which goes well beyond the customer-relationship management (CRM) recently in vogue with marketing people [3.35]. Such a service will go far beyond the simple signposting to a supplier that a broker might have provided historically. The conceptual basis for the relationship is more focused on clients' needs and details of their lifestyles and aspirations. ICT allows easier and quicker access to comprehensive and relevant information, provides greater precision in defining needs, is more flexible and will probably cost less.

These insights by Zuboff and Maxmin are particularly encouraging when coupled with Christensen's. They do not directly address the problems of truly sustainable growth but are not incompatible with the concept and the systemic change to capitalism advocated here. I would argue that more creative, non-materialistic ways of servicing people's needs is both a way of reducing material consumption and creating new types of employment without capital growth. If the distribution of work is more evenly spread we might also get a better balance between work and the rest of our lives. Rather than people being subordinate to the needs of capitalism, capitalism ought to meet the needs of people. Neglected families and broken communities are not what people need.

Impact

The impact of capitalism is truly global. It is the great driver of human activity. It enables individuals, corporations and governments to pursue self interest in exactly the way Adam Smith discerned. Few would argue against it being responsible for the explosion in material wealth and the high standard of living we enjoy in the industrialised world. On the other hand, money delivers nothing per se. Money has no intrinsic value. Without things of value – the material world, services, interpersonal relationships, love, passion, leisure and the infrastructures which actually deliver our standard of living – capitalism would do very little.

Unfortunately value has become synonymous with money and things which cannot be bought are increasingly seen as worthless. A high standard of living is not the same as a good quality of life. Stock markets, which emerged to facilitate investment and a wider distribution of wealth and employment, have now become money-making machines for the few. Governments pander to them with an unquestioning lack of moral concern because they provide a large source of tax revenue. Pimping perhaps? The Planet has simultaneously been taken for granted and poverty is often sidelined as no more than an embarrassment. The challenge is therefore to modify capitalism to respect the Planet and seriously tackle the distribution of work and wealth. Perhaps then, progress will not lead to extinction and we may continue to evolve despite our limitations.

Capitalism is the aggregated effect of individuals pursuing self interest within a niche which demands that we remain credit worthy (to survive in effect). It no longer works very well. A change which aligns the self interest of individuals with the self interest of the Planet and impoverished people, would however result in an aggregated effect which improves capitalism and our adopted niche. It would result in a more caring and sustainable *Big Society*.

There is nothing about capitalism in its current form to refute the hypothesis of Chapter 2.

Notes and references for chapter 3

3.1   *The price of gold reached 820 euro ($1118 or £714) per troy ounce in February 2010. The euro was at that time under threat because of the indebtedness and large budget deficits of Portugal, Ireland, Greece and Spain (PIGS) and the low confidence of global financial markets in the ability of Greece in particular, to pay its debts.*

3.2   Niall Ferguson, *The Ascent of Money: A Financial History of the World*, Penguin Press, 2008, ISBN 1594201927.

3.3   *On 13ᵗʰ September 2007, BBC business editor Robert Peston broke the story that Northern Rock was seeking emergency financial support from the Bank of England.*
Northern Rock had found itself unable to secure loans from other banks on the inter-bank lending market, the Libor, so the Bank of England had stepped in as lender of last resort. The news set in motion a run on the bank. With Northern Rock confirming it had agreed emergency funding with the Bank of England, telephone lines were jammed and the queues of savers rushing to empty their accounts grew.

Four days into the crisis and the run on the bank showed no sign of halting. Faith in British banking was being destroyed. The UK-wide panic that followed wasn't halted until the late afternoon of Monday, 17ᵗʰ September, when Chancellor of the Exchequer Alistair Darling stepped in to guarantee all deposits held by Northern Rock.
Adam Harcourt-Webster, BBC Money Programme, September, 2007.

3.4   *Waterwheels were invented long before intellectual property could be protected through patents but more than 30,000 were in use throughout the UK until superseded by the Boulton and Watt invention of the steam engine. They made money for those who could build them and considerably more for those who owned them. They made fortunes for entrepreneurs in the woollen and cotton industries of the seventeenth and eighteenth centuries. In turn, Stephenson's improvement of the steam engine and development of the locomotive to run on an iron railway, made fortunes for the cotton magnates of Manchester and Liverpool, spawned the global railway industry and changed the social structure of Britain.*

The simultaneous invention of the jet engine by Sir Frank Whittle and Dr. Hans von Ohain, each unaware of the others work, and the subsequent development of a practical jet engine was not something to which UK investors initially rushed to risk their money. But due to Whittle's persistence and the threat of losing the second world war, the engine was eventually deployed in military aircraft such as the Meteor and Whittle gained deserved recognition. It later entered civilian commercial service in the Comet, a beautiful aircraft which continued duty for coastal reconnaissance after a crash which damaged its reputation and led to it being withdrawn from civilian service. The Comet demonstrates just how difficult it is to innovate in some areas of application such as transport. The innovation has to be perfect the very first time. A difficult trick when, by its very nature, it embraces uncertainty. Who would wish to be a test pilot?

Rolls Royce and Pratt and Witney are the legacy of Whittle and von Ohain. They spend huge amounts of money in developing jet engines to outstrip the performance of the existing engines and meet the increasing demands of new ideas in air transport, achieve ever higher efficiencies while reducing noise and emissions. But will they get the contracts with the airframe companies such as Airbus and Boeing to justify the investment costs? Mostly they do, but in 1970 a hitch with innovative materials nearly caused a catastrophe for Rolls Royce. The search for the next big improvement or value-adding idea is very costly and not risk-free.

3.5 *Lehman Brothers, a 158-year-old investment bank with 24,000 employees, filed for Chapter 11 bankruptcy protection on 15th September, 2008. It had lent more money than it could repay with liabilities of $613 billion. Its problems came to light when the state-owned Korea Development Bank was considering the purchase of Lehman and, because of "difficulties", placed its talks with Lehman on hold. The value of Lehman shares immediately fell by 45% and other banks and institutions no longer felt able to trade with it. Lehman's were insolvent. Close to 100 hedge funds were using Lehman as their prime broker and relied largely on the firm for financing their own credit needs. As a result the hedge funds were forced to sit on large cash balances inhibiting further growth. Confidence in international and inter-bank lending fell dramatically because the real assets available to underpin the credit already released by the banks into the financial markets were grossly inadequate. This meant that if investors sought repayment of their investments they could not all be met. Unless confidence could be restored by increasing bank assets, investors would seek to be first in the queue for repayment (before assets disappeared)* leading to the collapse of the entire financial system. Governments around the world stepped in to recapitalise the major banks i.e. give or lend them taxpayers money. While the notion that they should be allowed to fail, the consequences, even in the USA which does not favour rescues and handouts, were too horrendous to contemplate.

3.6   Cheshire based ACAL Energy Ltd (ACAL Energy), has completed a £3.5m investment round to boost the development of its innovative low-cost, fuel-cell technology. Carbon Trust Investments led the funding round, along with Solvay SA, Porton Capital and a leading Japanese automotive corporation. ACAL Energy's FlowCath® technology avoids the use of platinum which is commonly used in fuel cells but is an expensive precious metal. Having simplified the fuel cell system, ACAL's technology promises improved durability and reliability. Additional funds are expected.

3.7   A financial journalist who pocketed nearly £41,000 by "cynically manipulating" the stock market was jailed for six months in February 2006. James Hipwell used the City Slickers column in the Daily Mirror to ramp up the value of shares in a "tip, buy and sell" scam. He bought low-price shares and then promoted them in his newspaper column. He sold them profitably following their consequential rise in price.

3.8   An example of a Credit Default Swap (CDS). An investment trust owns £1 million corporation bond issued by a private housing firm. Since there is a risk that the private housing firm may default on repayments, the investment trust chooses to buy a CDS from a hedge fund. The CDS is worth £1 million. The investment trust thence pays interest on this CDS of say 3%, thence making payments of £30,000 a year for the duration of the contract. If the private housing firm doesn't default, the hedge fund gains the interest from the investment bank and pays nothing out. It makes a simple profit. If the private housing firm does default, then the hedge fund has to pay compensation to the investment bank of £1 million, the value of the CDS. Therefore the hedge fund takes on a larger risk of having to pay £1million should the housing firm default. Notionally the hedge fund has an asset with a revenue stream.

3.9   Adam Smith, *An Inquiry into the Nature and Causes of the Wealth of Nations,* University Of Chicago Press, 1977, ISBN 0226763749.

3.10   O'Rourke, P. J., *On The wealth of Nations,* Grove Atlantic Inc., 2007, ISBN 978 1 84354 389 3.

3.11   Milton Friedman, *Capitalism and Freedom,* University of Chicago Press, 2002, ISBN 0226264211.

3.12   Keynes, J.M., *The General Theory of Employment, Interest and Money,* Cambridge University Press for Royal Economic Society, 1936.

3.13   Ben Fine, *Marx's "Capital",* Pluto Press, 2003, ISBN10: 0745320503.

3.14   *Three years after Russian divers thrust a rust-proof flag into the seabed below the North Pole, the country's Prime Minister, Vladimir Putin, wants to stake Russia's claim in the increasingly frantic battle for control of the Arctic's resources. Ironically the more the ice melts through climate change the more the region is opened up for oil and gas exploration.*
While Russia counts for the bulk of Arctic land, seven other states have land in Arctic territory: Canada, Denmark, the United States, Iceland, Norway, Sweden, and Finland. Of these, Russia, Canada, Denmark, Norway and the US, are all claiming jurisdiction over parts of the region. And the reason is simple: it could contain as much as a quarter of the world's undiscovered reserves of oil and gas.
Andy Rowell, Oil Change International, September, 2010.

3.15   *The de Havilland Comet was the world's first commercial jet airliner to reach production and service. Developed and manufactured by de Havilland, it first flew in 1949 and was considered a landmark in British aeronautical design. Early Comet models suffered from what was eventually identified as catastrophic metal fatigue, causing a string of well-publicised crashes and many fatalities. The Comet had to be withdrawn from service.*

3.16   *Failing to make "realistic budgetary provision" and "slowing down projects" resulted in the Ministry of Defence overspending by 3.3 billion pounds ($5.3 billion) in 2009-2010 financial year, Parliament's National Audit Office said in a new report.*
The NAO said that although the management of individual projects had improved in the previous financial year, bad financial planning had boosted

the bill for Britain's Typhoon warplanes by 2.7 billion pounds, while delays to a plan to build two aircraft carriers had raised costs by 650 million pounds. "Central departmental decisions were taken to balance the defence budget which had the effect of driving very significant additional cost and delay into the equipment programme; this represents poor value for money for the taxpayer," NAO head Amyas Morse said in a statement.
UK National Audit Office, 2010.

3.17   *Ten of the most overspent UK Government projects*

Project: NHS national IT programme
Budget £2.3bn
Current cost £12.6bn
Percentage overspent 450 per cent. Established in October 2002, under Alan Milburn, scheme to link 30,000 GPs in England to nearly 300 hospitals has been derided for huge costs and technical problems.

Project: 2012 Olympics
Budget £2.4bn
Current cost £9.3bn
Percentage overspent 289 per cent
The euphoria that greeted the decision to award London the 2012 Games has largely given way to concerns over spiralling costs.

Project: Astute Class submarine
Budget £2.5bn
Current cost £3.8bn
Percentage overspent 48 per cent
The order for three of next-generation nuclear fleet submarines for the Royal Navy was announced in 1997 and subsequently increased to four. Only one has yet arrived.

Project: Type 45 destroyer
Budget £5.4bn
Current cost £6.4bn
Percentage overspent 18 per cent
Highly impressive replacements for the Type 42 class, but dogged by delays and cost overruns.

Project: Nimrod MK4
Budget £2.8bn
Current cost £3.6bn
Percentage overspent 28 per cent
A fixed-price order for 21 Nimrod 2000 aircraft was placed in 1996, with an in-service date of 2003. The project was reviewed in May 2006.

Project: Ministry of Justice Libra case management system
Budget £146m
Current cost £487m
Percentage overspent 234 per cent
Contract to provide a IT system for magistrates' courts was awarded in 1998. MPs told it would be completed by October 2007 or, in a "worst-case scenario", March 2008. It wasn't.

Project: Ministry of Justice's P-Nomis offender management system
Budget £234m
Current cost £513m
Percentage overspent 119 per cent
A National Audit Office analysis concluded that "the value for money achieved by the project was poor".

Project: Pensions Transformation programme for DWP
Budget £429m
Current cost £598m
Percentage overspent 39 per cent
An NAO report subsequently criticised the delays and overspend.

Project: Central payment system for the DWP
Budget £90m
Current cost £178m
Percentage overspent 98 per cent
Now expected to be delivered in December next year, five years after its planned completion date of October 2006.

Project: A46 Improvement
Budget £157m
Current cost £220m
Percentage overspent 40.1 per cent

Source: Taxpayers' Alliance

3.18 *"Fundamental to the functioning of a market system is the fact that each individual economic entity works extraordinarily assiduously to preserve its solvency; it is such a critical part of the way a competitive, free-market system works. You have to have that as a central ingredient in the market place or it will not work.*

The question isn't whether or not competitive markets function perfectly. They do not. Regrettably there is nothing better. The crisis (the 2008 one) will happen again but it will be different. It's human nature. Unless somebody can find a way to change human nature we will have more crises. None of them will look like this (the 2008 one) because no two crises have anything in common except human nature."

Alan Greenspan, Chairman of the US Federal Reserve Board from 1987 to 2006, speaking on BBC2 television programme, *The love of money*, broadcast 17th September, 2009.

3.19 *"This is something (the 2008 crisis) we've seen over several hundred years. But the fact that we've seen it in the past and not been able to improve things is a worry. This is one of a long series of financial crises. It's been the biggest one perhaps ever? But it has come out of the same sort of problems we've seen in the past. People who think the world has changed, I'm afraid have not read history."*

Mervyn King, Governor of the Bank of England speaking on the BBC2 television programme, *The love of money*, broadcast 17th September, 2009.

3.20 *"The linear increase in record life expectancy for more than 165 years does not suggest a looming limit to human lifespan. If life expectancy were approaching a limit, some deceleration of progress would probably occur. Continued progress in the longest-living populations suggests we are not close to a limit and further rises in life expectancy seem likely........".*

Kaare Christensen, , Gabrielle Doblhammer, Roland Rau, Roland and James W.Vaupel, *Ageing populations: the challenges ahead",* The Lancet, 374, Issue 9696, 3rd October, 2009.

3.21 *The river Leen, between Papplewick and Linby in Nottinghamshire, was first harnessed for its water power as early as 1232. By the 18th century the river powered many mills to process cotton and one, the Old or Grange Mill,* *had a 40 feet diameter breast wheel. This was, one of the largest ever built yet it was supplemented in 1791 by James Watts' steam engine. At this and many other mills, great numbers of pauper children imported from the London workhouses, were employed. These children, drafted into industry to save public expense and as cheap labour, suffered from the industrial conditions. They worked extremely long hours, were badly fed and clothed and poorly housed. As a result many died and were laid to rest in the churchyards, mainly in unmarked graves. Life expectancy at the time was less than 30 years.*

3.22   *In 2007 the former chairman of Her Majesty's Revenue and Customs (HMRC), Paul Gray, resigned following the department's loss of millions of child benefit records. He was paid £137,000 for his departure.*
In 2008, David Higgins, the chief executive of the Olympic Delivery Authority, was paid a performance-related bonus of £205,000, despite the budget for the Games rising to over £9 billion.
Tax Payers' Alliance, Public Sector Rich List, November, 2008.

3.23   *Under rules introduced in 1987, civil servants who have worked for at least 20 years are entitled to a lump sum worth two years' salary if they take voluntary redundancy. For those whose redundancy is compulsory, the standard payment is worth three years' pay, while in some cases the pay-off can be worth as much as six years' salary. In 2009, 15,000 civil servants had been made redundant over three years, receiving almost £1 billion in severance payments. The average payout was £60,000 but some public servants received as much as £100,000. In one case, two Treasury mandarins shared £1.1 million in severance pay.*

3.24   *In 2010 the statutory redundancy payment for an ordinary UK employee who has served at least two years is, by law, calculated as between one and two weeks wages for each year served. Thus a person aged 35 years, earning £13,000 a year and having ten years' service, when made redundant, is entitled to receive £2,500.*

3.25   *Mill's famous formulation of utilitarianism is known as the "greatest-happiness principle". It holds that one must always act so as to produce the greatest happiness for the greatest number of people, within reason. Mill's major contribution to utilitarianism is his argument for the qualitative separation of pleasures. He argues that intellectual and moral pleasures are superior to more physical forms of pleasure.*

Mill, J.S.,*"Utilitarianism"*, 1863.

3.26   *"The 20ᵗʰ century was a century of redistribution of income. The 21ˢᵗ century could be a century of redistribution of work. Redistribution would spread work more evenly across populations and over the ages of life. Individuals could combine work, education, leisure and child-rearing in varying amounts at different ages. Preliminary evidence suggests that shortened working weeks over extended working lives might further contribute to increases in life expectancy and health."*
Christensen, Kaare and colleagues (see also *3.20*).

3.27   *Deming offers fourteen key principles for transforming business effectiveness.*
1. *Create constancy of purpose toward improvement of product and service, with the aim to become competitive and stay in business, and to provide jobs.*
2. *Adopt the new philosophy. We are in a new economic age. Western management must awaken to the challenge, must learn their responsibilities, and take on leadership for change.*
3. *Cease dependence on inspection to achieve quality. Eliminate the need for massive inspection by building quality into the product in the first place.*
4. *End the practice of awarding business on the basis of price tag. Instead, minimize total cost. Move towards a single supplier for any one item, on a long-term relationship of loyalty and trust.*
5. *Improve constantly and forever the system of production and service, to improve quality and productivity, and thus constantly decrease costs.*
6. *Institute training on the job.*
7. *Institute leadership (see Point 12 and Ch. 8 of "Out of the Crisis"). The aim of supervision should be to help people and machines and gadgets to do a better job. Supervision of management is in need of overhaul, as well as supervision of production workers.*
8. *Drive out fear, so that everyone may work effectively for the company. (See Ch. 3 of "Out of the Crisis")*
9. *Break down barriers between departments. People in research, design, sales, and production must work as a team, to foresee problems of production and in use that may be encountered with the product or service.*

10. *Eliminate slogans, exhortations, and targets for the work force asking for zero defects and new levels of productivity. Such exhortations only create adversarial relationships, as the bulk of the causes of low quality and low productivity belong to the system and thus lie beyond the power of the work force.*

11. *Eliminate work standards (quotas) on the factory floor. Substitute leadership. Eliminate management by objective. Eliminate management by numbers, numerical goals. Substitute leadership*

12. *Remove barriers that rob the hourly worker of his right to pride of workmanship. The responsibility of supervisors must be changed from sheer numbers to quality.*
    Remove barriers that rob people in management and in engineering of their right to pride of workmanship. This means, inter alia," abolishment of the annual or merit rating and of management by objective

13. *Institute a vigorous program of education and self-improvement.*

14. *Put everybody in the company to work to accomplish the transformation. The transformation is everybody's job.*

Deming, W. E., *Out of the Crisis,* MIT Press, 1986, ISBN 0-911379-01-0

3. 28   T. C. Edwin Cheng, T. C. E. Cheng, Susan Podolsky, P. Jarvis, *Just-in-time manufacturing: an introduction*, Springer, 1996, ISBN 0412 73540 7.

3.29   Porter, M. E., *Competitive Advantage,* The Free Press, 1985, ISBN 0-02-925090-0.

3.30   Michael Hammer and James Champy, *Reengineering the Corporation: A Manifesto for Business Revolution,* Harper Collins, 2003, ISBN 9780060559533.

3.31   *Original definition of business-process model of a manufacturing enterprise and examples of business-process improvements via IT implementations.*

David Rhodes, *Integration challenge for small and medium companies,* invited paper, Proceedings of British Production and Inventory Control Society Conference on Integration, November, 1988.

3.32   Womac, J. P., Jones, D.T. *Lean Thinking: Banish Waste and Create Wealth in Your Corporation*, Free Press, 2003, ISBN-10: 0743249275, ISBN-13: 978-0743249270.

3.33   Imai, <u>Masaaki.</u> *Gemba Kaizen: A Commonsense, Low-Cost Approach to Management,* McGraw-Hill, 1997, ISBN-10: 0070314462, ISBN-13: 978-0070314467.

3.34   Shoshona Zuboff and James Maxmin, *The support economy, Penguin Books,* 2002, ISBN 0-670-88736-6.

3.35   Don Peppers and Martha Rogers, *The One to One Future,* Currency Doubleday, 1996, ISBN-10: 0385485662, ISBN-13: 978-0385485661.

Chapter 4
The human niche

"Man is quite insane. He wouldn't know how to make a maggot, and he makes gods by the dozen."

Michel de Montaigne, French essayist, Essays (1580)

Capitalism is clearly an important feature of the human condition but are there others which could better claim to define our niche? If so, might they be exploited or possibly modified to meet the challenges of sustainability and poverty?

Testing the hypothesis

The Planet has been around for at least 4.5 billion years [4.1] and the ideas relating to evolution in Chapter 2 barely 200 years. From what we now know, biological evolution of our species over the critical period of the next 100 years is unlikely to be significant or even detectable. What is more important is the evolution of the human condition and the hypothesis in Chapter 2 that we have created a powerful niche called capitalism, to which we individually, and through our many and various forms of organisation and government structures, have globally adapted.

The concern is that our adaptations to this synthetic niche are inadequate and/or inappropriate to survival as the wider environmental niche changes. The niche we have created has led us to relative complacency and indifference to global poverty, the emerging forces of climate change and the increasing scarcity of natural resources.

The significance of this hypothesis is so great as to require testing. As Popper explains in his philosophy of science, an hypothesis may claim to be scientific if a test can be devised which might refute it. The scientific method is thence to accept an hypothesis until it is refuted, or until a better hypothesis which extends and encompasses the original comes along [4.2]. So let us look at the human niche to see where else we might look for evolutionary change and refutation of this hypothesis.

Occupants of our niche

The range of humankinds' constituent social, political and economic organisations, groups and systems is legion. They include quasi-global organisations such as the United Nations as well as individual countries, nations, states, cities, towns, villages, tribes, regional bodies such as the European Union, the world's great religions, the not so great religions, industries, commercial enterprises, trade unions, political parties, professional bodies, voluntary organisations, educational establishments, charities, sports clubs and arts societies plus truly countless others including the family.

I have gathered together many of these under the headings below in a crude attempt to classify the kinds of features which describe humankind as a whole. In their detailed manifestations they are all evolving and may therefore help us get a grip on the drivers of evolution. Evolution in this sense is easy to accept since it is observable during one's own lifespan and the history lessons at school. It is simply a generalisation of the historic examples set out in the opening to Chapter 2.

(a) Law (e.g. principles, methods of administering justice, ownership)

(b) Organisational structures (e.g. tribes, city and nation states, businesses, institutions, armed services, social groups, sports bodies)

(c) Political systems (e.g. leaders, monarchies, despots, democracies)

(d) Belief systems (e.g. religious, secular, agnostic, scientific, ritualistic, philosophical, class-based)

(e) Education (e.g. based on theory, religious knowledge, skills, customs or doctrines)

(f) Social responsibility (e.g. based on state, religion, community, family or individual)

(g) Resources (e.g. water, food, energy, mineral, natural and recycled forms)

    (h) Technology (e.g. artefacts, weaponry, medicine, dwellings, transport and communications)

    (i) Systems of exchange (e.g. currency, markets and terms of trade)

Undoubtedly some readers will disagree with my choices, but I wouldn't defend a particular set very strongly since the constituents are not necessarily independent anyway and alternative classifications are certainly possible. Religious beliefs, for example, may well determine the political and education systems in some countries; resources may influence organisational structures, artefacts and systems of exchange. Defence might warrant a separate heading? The inherent fuzziness surrounding the list is important. It admits to the fundamental complexity of humankind which is that we can really only assert that it consists of things (such as people, organisations and resources) and connections between things (such as relationships, transactions and the exchange of information). With its seven continents, five oceans and population approaching seven billion people, the range of "things" and numbers of "connections" to be found on our planet defies simple definition. Nothing exists without some kind of connection with something else and everything on the Planet is connected directly or indirectly to everything else (see Chapter 5). For the moment let us settle on the human condition being very complex. It is evolving but is it evolving towards extinction or survival?

Bounded rationality

In 1961 Herbert Simon was awarded a Nobel prize for his work and insight into what he called "bounded rationality" [4.3, 4.4]. This is his observation that the human brain and cognitive ability is limited and therefore the comprehension of even the greatest minds falls short of understanding everything. And even without bounded rationality, the totality of the knowledge present in the minds of the human race, its libraries, organisations and artefacts is limited. Human cognition is also flawed because the human race is still learning and its perceptions are constrained by its abilities to sense and perceive. One person's perception and version of knowledge is often different from another's even within a given field of expertise.

Sadly, bounded rationality, when it has been heard of at all, is widely accepted as a self-evident simple point with little utility. But you don't get a Nobel prize for simple observations with no utility. It is actually extremely relevant to the human condition and a hugely important element in life and fundamental to the arguments put forward in this book.

Bounded rationality tells us that any one person or group cannot specify a set of organisations or political structures to better suit humankind based on their knowledge. Their knowledge will always be inadequate.

Bounded rationality means it is impossible for any human, or group of humans, to sufficiently comprehend the totality of global activity as to thence intervene with any certainty of the aggregated outcomes.

Traditions

Nonetheless, the consequences of bounded rationality don't preclude individuals trying to improve our understanding of what defines the human condition and makes it "tick". For example, Feyerband is among those who have attempted to make sense of it all under the general guise of "traditions" and expresses a concern for them and their relationships [4.5]. It is all rather heavy stuff and, since any message intended to have universal influence will more easily take root if it is simple, immediately confirms the difficulties facing us. Traditions clearly exist. A tradition (or subculture) is a rather vague concept but can be defined for the purpose of this discussion as "a group of relationships and people (i.e. connections and things), which have sufficient commonality of belief, aspiration or practice, to be identifiable and hence labelled as unique". For example "Christians", "Luddites", "The Labour Party", "Athletes", "Thugs", "Medics", "Humanists", "Technologists" and so on. Any individual may also be a component in any number of different traditions.

Feyerband points out that such traditions are diverse and often the cause of conflict when, as is often the case, they strive for dominance. To reconcile such diversity he looks at the matter of how traditions coexist in society as a whole and what society itself might be. He concludes that a free society is the goal and that a free society is one in which all traditions have equal rights and access to the centres of power. This differs from what he sees as the customary definition where individuals have equal rights of access to positions defined by a special tradition, usually one defined by intellectuals or experts such as the tradition of western technology. I quote his view: "a tradition receives its rights not because of the importance (cash value, as it were) it has for outsiders but because it gives meaning to those who participate in it. But it can also be of value to outsiders. For example, some forms of tribal medicine may have better ways of diagnosing and treating (mental and physical) illness than scientific medicine of today and some primitive cosmologies may help us to see predominant views from a more detached and less hyperbolic perspective. To give traditions equality is therefore not only right but useful."

He develops these ideas and how a free society may be realised but, above all, avoids the idea that there is some overarching theory which if only it could be found would enable all traditions to somehow coexist in one, happily combined tradition. Such a theory would, he says, simply be another tradition dominating our lives and "turn living human beings into well-trained slaves of their own barren vision of life." In this he is not alone as evidenced in the UK by the ever increasing intervention of the state through both laws [4.6] and surveillance [4.7]. If not exactly enslaving they are arguably steps in that undesirable direction. His vision is of a much more lively evolution of traditions, changing not static. "They will reflect what people want and what they are, they will also be more flexible, better adapted to particular problems than what sociologists (Marxist, Parsonians etc.), political scientists or just any intellectual may dream up in their offices".

These remarks are somewhat chastening since this book is very close to a synthesis of what others and I have "dreamed up". But he too has set out (i.e. dreamed up) an intellectual manifesto and anyway, isn't there always a case for considering new ideas and innovations on merit regardless of their provenance? Isn't this book just another set of ideas which might emerge to be one of his "lively traditions"? Overall, his views appear to resonate with Popper's belief in self-liberation and the general desire for an open society [4.8], so I suspect we are all on the same side. If anything he is guilty of assuming an infinitely bountiful planet and therefore underestimates the additional aggravation of how traditions share limited resources without conflict. He may not be able to envisage a universal tradition but in reality the Planet's population already share the universal tradition of "free-market capitalism" and even if they do not accept or realise it, our one and only Planet's limited resources. However, like Popper he sees variety and choice at the grass roots of society as components in the evolutionary path to survival; perhaps that increasing variety suggested by Ashby's Law.

His message is clear - intervention must respect and not confound the aspiration to attain a free and open society. But he doesn't say what the intervention should be.

So the hypothesis of Chapter 2 is consistent with Feyerband's and Popper's belief in a free and open society. A systemic change to the one overarching system we seem to be stuck with (capitalism) would apply to everyone equally. It would alter the niche but leave traditions to continue evolving towards their different visions of society – the *Big Society*.

Religions and beliefs

Is there perhaps some universally-defining feature other than capitalism which embraces the human race? Well, religion is a possibility. Religions seem to be widely held by most of the world's population to be custodians of beliefs even if each one is only able to believe in its own. They define what people should believe and there are alternative religions to accommodate our different views. Unfortunately religions have a poor track record of collaboration as every national newspaper frequently reports. They give rise to political tension and conflicts as currently illustrated in Afghanistan, Iraq, Pakistan and Iran - albeit mixed up with calls for freedom and democracy and undermined by corruption. The major religions share similar values nonetheless and maybe there is hope in that. Such universal values as "do as you would be done to" are, incidentally, not the sole preserve of religions and may simply be the outcome of the evolutionary selection process because that particular "value" often favours one's survival.

Any tradition is keen to preserve its identity and demands loyalty from its members just like a club. Clubs revel in their differences. Big clubs enjoy the power they have over their members and the members enjoy being identified with a powerful club. So when a religion transcends many countries its leaders enjoy a lot of power and have a considerable incentive to maintain its exclusivity. This phenomenon of achieving power through religion is most obvious in those countries such as Saudi Arabia where "the club and its rules" are not just exclusive but obligatory and synonymous with government and the rule of law.

Even Christians remain divided. During my lifetime Roman Catholics in Britain were at one stage not allowed to marry Anglicans without the Anglican in question committing to Catholicism. Jewish and Roman

Catholic pupils at my Church of England primary school were excused the morning assembly because, I presumed, the "wrong" prayers were said and the "wrong" hymns sung. As an adult I can see that it was more to do with "arm wrestling" and demonstration of religious strength. Muslims, Christians and Jews share the same God but you need to enquire to find this out since it isn't obvious from their public stance. Even the Church of England has managed to divide itself into sects and some will still make much of being either "Chapel" or "Church".

It is difficult, as an engineer I would say impossible, to accept the views of religious fanatics who believe both that they know the unknowable and should impose their belief on others. To state and even promote a belief may be reasonable but to impose it on others, incite intolerance of alternative beliefs or oppose them violently seems totally unacceptable (and irrational). The Universe of which the solar system and our Planet are a part, is considered to be around 156 billion light years wide [4.9]. This is difficult to comprehend. 156 billion is 156,000,000,000 and might just be imaginable within the human compass. But this number must be multiplied by 5,860,000,000,000 to obtain the width of the Universe in miles. On such a scale we and our planet are as close to a practical definition of infinitesimally small as one might wish. As individuals we must be close to insignificant. One cannot but wonder at it all and reflect upon our ignorance and the veracity of our beliefs.

It is encouraging therefore that it appears possible to eradicate religious conflict and intolerance. Until recently it was almost eradicated in Europe and the Americas. So the fact that religious intolerance is surfacing again, principally as a confrontation between small groups of fundamentalists of various kinds but with a fair dose of anti-Semitism from non-believers too, is profoundly sad. Such conflict, when embraced by a nuclear state could easily escalate to destroy humankind.

There are also secular beliefs. In his recent book, Stephen Hawking believes he can explain the origins and evolution of the universe, including ourselves, mathematically [4.10]. Richard Dawkins appears to believe as passionately about science as others do about religion [4.11] and a judge at a recent court case ruled that an employee who holds strongly held views based on science should receive the same legal consideration in regard to those views as someone with a particular religious belief [4.12].

One should be careful about accepting even science as the ultimate truth. The sun may be expected to rise tomorrow largely because it has done so for several billion years. Yet its rise is only a probability not a certainty.

All technologists implicitly hold a belief in the utility of science but, unlike religious beliefs, not in the absolute truth of scientific knowledge per se. Popper's definition of scientific knowledge states that scientific knowledge is open to improvement. In this lies much humility and wisdom which contrasts dramatically with beliefs such as those being promoted by creationists, followers of the intelligent-design (ID) movement in the USA and to a lesser extent the UK. These people believe that God created the world around 6000 years ago; that the evidence for such a feat and such a god is that human and other life forms are too complex to have evolved and must have been designed "intelligently".

As a belief it is perhaps as good as, and no worse than, many others. But the disciples of this belief claim it as science and wish to see it taught as science rather than a religious belief. It is highly controversial and is being taught as science in some US schools. The dispute goes back many years to the Monkey trial of 1925 when John Scopes was convicted of teaching Darwin's theory of evolution contrary to state law. The law was based on the literal interpretation of the biblical explanation of the creation [4.13].

When scientific knowledge is shown to be inadequate it is invariably due to an improved theory and simply adds to our understanding. In his book on "The Nature of Scientific Revolutions" Kuhn explains that at any one time in history a scientific theory was accepted if it explained the evidence and was useful [4.14]. Subsequent theories were often rejected by the incumbent exponents of a widely-held theory until a revolution in thinking could be brought about by a new generation of scientists and thinkers. The key point, also echoed by Popper, is that a subsequent theory has to explain what the previous theory explained and more [4.2]. The supposed identification of a gas to explain combustion, which scientists called phlogiston was a helpful "discovery" for scientists in the 17th century. Today schoolboys see phlogiston as a joke because we have since "discovered" the elements, the periodic table, oxygen and the process of oxidation (burning). In another 200 years contemporary theories may in turn seem like a joke but they are undoubtedly useful to us in our time.

A superseded theory may even continue to be applicable for the more limited range of conditions to which it is found to correspond. For example, Einstein's theories improved on Newton's theories of mechanics and gravitation but we still use Newton's theories a lot. This is because for the majority of day-to-day circumstances Newton's theories remain sufficiently accurate to yield answers much more easily than Einstein's. And of course we understand when Einstein's should be used rather than Newton's.

With the important exception of scientific knowledge and the definition by which it (and engineering and technology) is distinguished from all other knowledge, beliefs are not universal. It is thus unlikely, even impossible, that religion holds the key to adapting our niche. The increasing probability that some extremist religious group could obtain nuclear weapons and thence use them against huge numbers of "non-believers" suggests religion might even endanger it.

But if we are considering systemic change, religions illustrate one very relevant and important point. In the middle ages Europe was dominated by religion. The Roman Catholic Church ruled through fear. Hell and damnation awaited anyone who challenged its dictates. Almost everyone in the population behaved as the Church decreed because the decrees were effectively systemic. Non-conformers were called heretics and nasty consequences kept the numbers down to a very small minority. In our secular society this no longer applies and it is capitalism and what is legal that determines people's behaviour. In Saudi Arabia, Iran and much of Asia, religious belief still provides a strong systemic constraint on individuals and communities.

Philosophy

Maybe philosophy transcends the whole of humankind and contains some universal truth we can agree on? Unfortunately philosophy is largely impenetrable to most people and has become the preserve of specialists. In its raw form it does not appear to provide solutions but it might provide some clues. It purports to seek and understand what lies within us and can make a credible claim to be founded on reason rather than faith. Socrates believed that philosophy is more about understanding how we ought to live than understanding nature (science) although many disagree. There are therefore many strands of philosophy with differences and passions just as strong as those between religions [4.15]. As a means of changing our niche, philosophy makes a poor start.

Nevertheless, it may help our understanding. Hegel's philosophy is an encouraging example [4.16]. According to him it was Socrates who undermined and subverted the harmony of the Athenians because he asked questions which they found difficulty in answering, such as "What is justice?" and "What is virtue?" As a result, instead of a daily life, which for the average Athenian was a simple matter of following state custom and practice and was "very nice thank you", the consciousness of Athenian society was awakened to embark on a period of conflict and turmoil. Hegel derived from this his theory that historical developments were a significant part of philosophy and identified what he called the process of "dialectical change". This is the phenomenon through which periods of social stability, such as the Athenian way of life before Socrates and the European experiences before the two world wars, is challenged and destabilised by new ideas which inevitably cause conflict. Then, after a period, the conflicts are resolved and stability of a new kind is achieved. In due course yet newer ideas emerge, relevant to the then status quo, and the process is repeated.

This process of dialectic-change Hegel asserted, has three stages: thesis, antithesis and synthesis. Thesis is a stable state of affairs accepted over a period of time, antithesis is the challenge brought about by new ideas, and synthesis is the period during which conflicts are resolved to result in another thesis. Of course, the question arises as to whether this process is leading anywhere in particular and presents a rich field upon which philosophers can reflect. Popper, for example, believed that Hegel was "wrongheaded" and that there are no hidden meanings in history, that there is no ethical or moral goal to which history is directed. But Hegel believed that the process has a goal and ultimately leads to a final state of harmony in which conflicts such as those between reason and desire, morality and self-interest are reconciled in essentially a spiritual consensus. Today it is a reasonable guess that he would, with some difficulty, also have to include the sustainability of the planet in the process's goals.

The practical significance of Hegel's view is that Marx picked up his ideas and used many of them in what was to become known as Marxism [3.14]. Under the influence of Marxism, more than 50 years of communism gives credence to the idea that change can be brought about by the dialectic process and the espousing of new ideas. However it was hardly the reconciliation of complex moral and selfish issues that Hegel leads us to suppose would ensue, and the dialectic process may be more obvious in hindsight than it had been in prospect. There may also have been much more of what Popper sees as significant in contemporary society, that emancipation, the self-liberation through knowledge, is a major driver of change and that an open society is the goal of almost all of us.

Hegel seems to have made a valid point nonetheless. Russia under the Romanovs was, however hard on the majority, a state of thesis. The 1917 revolution was the culmination of a short period of antithesis and was followed by a period of synthesis including Stalin's purges. Thesis thence describes the 50 years or so of authoritarian, socialist, state-planned economics of the USSR and its satellites. But, failing economic, social and political processes compared unfavourably with the democratic, free-market alternative evident in the USA, Japan and Europe. The consequence was a further period of antithesis which climaxed in the fall of the Berlin wall and dissolution of the USSR. Synthesis is again in progress as the individual states resulting from the dissolution get to grips with democracy and free-market economics. Technology and capital nonetheless existed in the old USSR and while marginally inferior, the technologies evolved just as they did in the USA, Japan and Europe. The soviets were into space ahead of the USA and were also a contemporary nuclear power alongside them, France and the UK.

Maybe we can draw hope from all this. Since communism was able to achieve the redirection of half a continent in less than 50 years we might just manage to succeed in addressing climate change globally. We may just be in a period of antithesis, waiting for the necessary consensus ahead of a full-blooded acceptance of the steps needed for a satisfactory synthesis and thesis. Of course the interpretation of the word "satisfactory" is somewhat subjective. Millions died in Robespiere's France, Hitler's Germany, Stalin's Russia and Pohl Pot's Cambodia. It seems that in matters of philosophy we should take great care before leaping from the intellectual to the practical.

Philosophy clearly informs but is not widely agreed or understood; it does not define the human condition and sufficient consensus about our niche and how it should change is not evident.

Science, engineering and technology

Our niche is certainly littered with evidence of science, engineering and technology so do they define us? No. They have, can and will deliver much. They already have the capability to deliver mitigating and adaptive solutions to climate change (see Chapter 6). They have demonstrably led to the economic success of the so-called developed world but have failed to do the same in the under-developed world. Or perhaps they have not been available to the latter who have either been unable to develop transforming technologies or their leaders have deemed them unnecessary.

Here I feel compelled to declare a caveat about using the word "developed" and have similar reservations about "civilised" and "industrialised" too. All convey the idea of something progressive and therefore good yet all have retrogressive and undesirable features. Nonetheless the terms are widely used in relation to particular countries and are so used here.

Feyerband includes "science" among his traditions and states that technology (he uses the word science but with the same meaning and intent) is characteristic of a whole set of what are collectively "intellectual traditions". This carries with it the possibility that, like many other traditions, it may be taken or left according to the disposition of society. But technology is not just any tradition held by a subsection of humankind, intellectual or otherwise. Water boils in predictably the same way wherever you may find it. Snake venom is not an opinion nor a point of view. A bicycle operates the same in any country, does not converse but provides transport regardless of gender, race or religion. The translation of energy from one form to another is explainable by the laws of thermodynamics and may be trusted in the design of many life-enhancing artefacts. People may not be aware of it, but entropy happily increases independently of any human intervention. Technology, especially the science on which it is based, is a universal reality, a tradition if you like, but one which transcends all other traditions. Scientific knowledge exists independently of humankind. Yet, in its practical manifestation for billions of people alive today, the withdrawal of technology would be catastrophic and lead to many deaths.

It is of course arguable, even likely, that if the global population were much smaller and its use of technology more selective, humankind might well be better off. But this is not a choice. The genie is out of the box. The reality is that the application of technical knowledge has helped many of us to live in comfort, produce wealth and create the spare time to enjoy leisure, help others, aspire, dream and create. For many of us it eliminates the drudgery of the otherwise full-time struggle to survive and allows many different traditions to develop. But these benefits are all conditional on whether we can afford them. Little is created outside the arts and sport unless it can be sold for a profit. Even charities require funds to purchase the technology needed to engage with contemporary life.

Engineering, science and technology are essential to our survival. They embody the means to adapt but do not of themselves change our niche nor refute the hypothesis. Their ability to do these things is contingent on meeting the demands of the capitalist system, that is making a profit. Unfortunately, technological solutions for climate-change mitigation and adaption do not offer a more profitable solution in comparison with previously accepted ways of doing things. Mitigation and adaption do not have obvious and immediate monetary value and sustainable methods are almost always complicated and initially expensive. In fact almost all appropriate measures incur increased costs. As for reducing poverty – where's the (financial) benefit in that?

Education and culture

Education is self-evidently important. How else would we share and spread new knowledge and provide individuals with enough nous to make life-affecting decisions. Democracy is strengthened when voters are able to question and scrutinise what their leaders would have them suppose. Maybe education is therefore a defining feature?

Technology, education and culture are of course inextricably linked. It is through education and dissemination that good ideas are communicated and exploited. Stephenson may have designed and built the first commercial locomotive but it took thousands of drivers and trains to create a railway which could meet the daily needs of millions. A modern locomotive driver requires extensive education and training before he can aspire to join the workforce of thousands of others, each of whom must be trained to take responsibility for the hundreds of passengers carried at speeds exceeding 200 km per hour. Each of whom obtains an income from this work which in turn passes to shops, their suppliers and the social life of the wider community. In the early days of steam locomotion, the railway routines determined the patterns of daily life way beyond the railway itself and railway anecdotes become the stuff of conversation and jokes. Skilled individuals and big personalities emerged to provide the leadership and role models for the young and in such highly complex ways "cultures are formed and defined" in railway towns such as Crewe, Darlington, Derby, Shildon and Swindon.

Computer technology has had a recent, similar and powerful effect. Computers would be useless without the well educated and trained installation and maintenance technicians, without the highly educated society and infrastructure which in turn provide and support them. Any modern economy would founder without these things because computers and communications technologies are essential to every branch of commerce in our competitive world. Yet, in the early days of personal computers when only a few people understood them and their potential, a lack of education meant that their exploitation was seriously delayed. What people do not understand they are inclined to fear.

The impact is not restricted to commerce. How amazing it is that so many people over 80 can use computers for word processing, internet searches and email. They routinely set their television recorders and use mobile phones with alacrity. Yet, at primary school they probably used slates (paper was too expensive.), wrote copper-plate handwriting and in their first 20 years were unlikely to have had used a telephone. Their personal development is because of a culture which embraces technology and excludes those who won't or don't participate.

Culturally, television and internet technology have created the means by which people need hardly ever meet another human being. It is possible to work from home, shop via the internet, receive deliveries at one's own door, engage with others via social networking web sites and receive all manner of entertainment from television sets with a choice of hundreds of channels. Physical engagement with others in the local community is diminishing with potentially undesirable consequences for social cohesion, community self-help and care.

My humble lineage is a microcosmic example of how technology, education and culture march together.

- Great grandfather (b. 1830) – education unknown but could read and write as the seventh son of a weaver/clothier; a hedger and ditcher working on the land in the agricultural economy, nine children, lived in two rooms.
- Grandfather (b. 1881) – formally educated to 14, worked as a gardener initially but became a driver and mechanic when the internal combustion engine replaced the horse, employed by an entrepreneur running an innovative bus company during

transition from land to an industrial economy, three children, lived in a simple, stone-built, terraced house in a mining community with radio but no telephone.

- Father (b. 1912) – grammar-school educated to 16, skilled technician for engineered products and later general manager in the mass-production, factory economy, three children, rented a semi-detached house on a privately-owned housing estate, with land-line telephone and television.

- Myself (b. 1939) – grammar-school and university educated to 25+, engineering, computing and management skills, engaged in the energy and information economies, three children, wife also university-educated and an engineering professional, own house in smart suburb, with broadband internet, networked computers for home and work, cable and free-view television, mobile and land-line telephones.

Education is, however, difficult to define. Lord Broers is seriously concerned with the narrow education the UK provides for its students [4.17]. There is also a huge variation in the ability of any one individual to assimilate whatever discipline it might be. At one end of the scale we have individuals who have simply been indoctrinated [4.18] and at the other, well-rounded individuals who can think and learn for themselves. In between there is the transfer of skills in such things as computer programming, foreign languages, medical diagnosis and vehicle maintenance. But to be innovative and really useful other skills such as problem-solving and thinking for oneself are, at the very least, desirable.

Knowledge acquisition is more than information and skills transfer. It is a process. Some knowledge may be acquired at anytime, other knowledge requires the sequential development of an ever-increasing body of knowledge and skills over time. For example, it's necessary to have a sound knowledge of mathematics and physics to study advanced engineering and these in themselves need several years of progressive (and successful) study.

There is a distinction too between knowing something (as in knowledge of individual facts or items of information), in understanding concepts and theory (inter-relationships and dependencies), knowing how to do something (theory and processes) and being able to do it (intellectual, creative, practical , managerial and social skills).

Training is an especially important class of education because it focuses on the development of a well-defined skill for carrying out a task (process) successfully. If the task is well defined it is possible to train people to do it without them necessarily understanding the theory; what exactly it's all about. In this way for example, assembly lines of cars produce millions of near fault-free vehicles using a work force split into small teams with limited but high-competences in just one aspect of car manufacture. This is achieved by the division of labour and training. It also acknowledges that it is unlikely that anyone on their own would be able to produce an entire vehicle from scratch to the quality customers require.

Education is self-evidently very dependent on the person being educated. Turn only to your school chums to witness the diversity with which they assimilated and took forward notionally the same education. Most insidious of all is the education we receive from life's experiences starting at the moment we are born. Some is subliminal; we simply respond to that environment and those in it. Some is more overt and reflects the variety in the strengths and weaknesses of the human race. We mostly feel pressure to conform and non-conformity is often discouraged. It takes time and experience to realise that our ideas may be rejected because they threaten vested interests and not necessarily because they lack merit; that innovation and change are thus often difficult to bring about.

Nobel prize winner and free-thinker, Dorothy Lessing, expresses this very eloquently in the preface to her novel "The Golden Notebook". She has some hard things to say about the ways we educate, or rather inculcate, our children and define values in the developed world and convinces me that education in this sense is not the totally progressive affair we might at first suppose [4.19]. It confirms that the challenge to persuade people to understand and address the weaknesses in how we currently live our lives is considerable. It illustrates that education is not straightforward and pure.

And another link between education and technology, again attributable to Popper [4.20], is that universities, schools, books, libraries and internet are not the only sources of knowledge. That motor car standing in the drive embodies the knowledge which went into creating it. It is the manifestation of human knowledge and, if by some odd chance humankind evaporated, our cars and billions of other artefacts which remained would inherently retain that "knowledge".

Clearly education has a major role in the development of the human condition. But it is not in itself sufficiently well defined or predicable in its outcomes to be a definition of our niche.

Politics

A suggested way of changing the niche called capitalism may be found in "Capitalism Matters" by Jonathan Porritt [4.21]. This book is perhaps what one would expect of the co-founder of Forum for the Future. As a broadcaster and commentator on sustainable development he argues that appropriate policies offer a route to genuine progress (survival). I admire the quality of his argument and the visibility he creates. I agree with his assertion that "It is all but impossible to deny any longer the need for profound change in the face of today's gathering ecological crisis". His view that "capitalism is so embedded in the human psyche as desirable that it is impractical to remove it" simply reinforces the hypothesis.

But I have reservations when he sets out positive suggestions for policies under what he defines as the "five capitals" – natural, human, manufactured, financial and social. Much as I admire the sentiments and his objectives, his suggestions are essentially all top-down. There is no new concept, it is business as usual but with "better" policies. Unfortunately, policies are not actions. We get a plethora of "better" policies ahead of any election and are invariably disappointed once our votes have been counted. This is because the retention of political power favours the most urgent and populist measures. One can be certain that when the Thames is lapping inside the Houses of Parliament, bees are no longer able to pollinate our crops and half the population is shivering or worse through lack of fuel, that "better" policies will be implemented. Then will be too late and the Planet so hot that catastrophe will be inevitable.

Politics are a universal phenomenon but not universal in kind. In themselves they are simply inadequate. Aside from the problem of achieving continuous political consensus across a wide range of fiscally complex matters, which is difficult to achieve on a global scale, they depend for their efficacy on a top-down approach. This runs counter to the very point made at the beginning of this chapter, that such an approach is confounded by the "bounded rationality" of humans and their inability to comprehend the scale of the complexity (see Chapter 5). Top-down control is impractical to agree and maintain on a global scale. Any purely policy-based initiative, however global, cannot provide the requisite variety to meet the ever increasing complexity of the environment in which we live (see also Ashby's Law [2.13]). We need politics to achieve the required systemic change to capitalism but we cannot rely on politics for the solution per se.

The law

"Thou shalt not kill" is a good example of a universally acceptable law, at least at the level of personal morality and in the tenets of all the great religions. It is a systemic, accepted feature of everyone's daily life. Yet millions are killed every year in the name of some cause or other because the leaders give dispensation to their followers to kill non-believers or whichever enemy they designate. The British people and UK laws continue to support Government-authorised actions by our armed forces who kill many individuals every year and are themselves killed by others.

It is against the law in the UK to cycle or park on pedestrian pavements, yet millions do so with impunity because it is impractical to enforce laws which so many people consider inappropriate. When I was a child, the death penalty applied to those who were convicted of murder and it was against the law to take part in a homosexual act even in private. The law has since been changed and progressively relaxed. Capital punishment no longer applies for murder and homosexuality has reached the point at which the law (and society) allows same sex marriages.

These examples illustrate that the law requires the consent of the majority and is largely a matter of public attitudes and culture which are naturally subject to changes over time.

The law is of course essential and a useful tool. It is undoubtedly a desirable feature of the human condition and arguably one of our most civilizing influences. In support of the law one can invoke Adam Smith's observation that self interest is crucially important in harnessing the motivation and energies of human beings. Consequently, where it clearly supports the self-interest of any one individual by placing constraints on all individuals, the law stands a good chance of being acceptable and enforceable. It would thus appear to be a universal feature of the human condition. But it is not in itself a definition of our niche but an adjunct to constrain our behaviour. The law must be applied to something since it is not in itself a behaviour or activity. The law already supports the current capitalist system in that the great majority of individuals and organisations already trust the major currencies, the mechanisms for their exchange and the long-established practices in regard to contracts. Theft and fraud are crimes.

The law could thus help to create a systemic change to capitalism but does not in itself suggest or define that change.

David Rhodes

Leadership

Leadership is close to politics. It is self-evident today and from history that leaders are important, especially when they are bad. Without recourse to any books most of us could immediately list hundreds. Ghandi, Ghengis Khan, Alexander the Great, Churchill, Elizabeth I, Cromwell, Hitler, Saddam Hussein, President Kennedy, De Gaulle, Margaret Thatcher and Angela Merkel - straight from my head with no thought of relative success or importance but, as I reflect on them, mostly national and political it seems. Another important list might be of intellectual pace setters such as Pythagoras, Euclid, Galileo, Newton, Descartes, Faraday and Einstein, or perhaps Shakespeare, Turner, Picasso, Moore, Hepworth, Knight, Sutherland and Dali. And of course the leaders in sport, music, technology, the law and in all aspects and levels of daily life.

But leaders are mortal and of their generation. They are a feature of humankind but not a definition. They are often created by the exigencies of their time as for example Churchill, who famously said he was born for his role in the second world war. Thatcher limited the excesses of trade unions and Cromwell did most of us a favour by limiting the power of the monarchy. Ghandi was the right man for India when the British Empire was beginning to sag as was Nasser in giving Egypt its self esteem. But even the British Empire, the greatest the world has ever seen, occupied only a fraction of the planet and it wasn't dominated by one man but by a culture of which Queen Victoria was only the titular head. A culture which had a great many subsidiary leaders who aspired to imperialism at a time when Britain was socially, economically, militarily and technologically well suited to the task of building an empire – from gunboats to tin trays, tiffin and gin. The fact that, to underpin imperial success, huge numbers of British children and adults were simultaneously living in poverty and working for often 14 hours a day in dangerous factories and disease-ridden slums, is often overlooked. Some leadership!

For all his influence, Mao's socialist ideals and leadership, the China of 30 years ago is nothing like the China of today. The standard of living in Beijing is, for many, now much the same as London, Paris or New York. The majority of people around the world, even in the poorest countries, wisely or possibly foolishly, share an aspiration which is to enjoy the standard of living and quality of life they see in the industrialised nations.

People are led and inspired not just by leaders but by what they see around them, on television and through other media.

Nelson and Wellington are acknowledged as two of the greatest military leaders Britain has ever produced but whether or not they had defeated Napoleon is hardly likely to have seriously altered the course of change to the human condition in Europe. Had Napoleon won, Mrs Smith and Monsieur Legrange may have had very different experiences even to the numbers of their offspring. Our religious preferences and legal system might now be French. Nevertheless it is difficult to argue that this would have prevented the advent of motor cars, roads, steam engines, aircraft, telephones, computers, televisions, contraceptives or synthetic fibres, to list but a few of what we today take for granted. Technology would have developed anyway, the nature of work and daily life would have been largely defined by capitalism and we would still have global warming.

Nelson's victories were clearly down to his leadership but enabled by technology. At Trafalgar he beat a numerically superior force by manoeuvring his ships more effectively and getting more shots per minute out of his guns than the French and Spanish. He deployed the same technology but to better effect since he'd been practicing at sea for months while the French and Spanish were confined to harbour. Had the French or Spanish had better technology, for example a type 45 destroyer such as HMS Daring recently supplied to the British Navy [4.22], they would have eliminated Nelson's fleet without receiving a single hit, and with (only?) a captain in charge.

As Darwin and Koestler have already observed, evolution of the human condition is progress to ever greater complexity and thus inherently very complex. As Simon explains, it isn't in its totality comprehensible to any one person. It is therefore unrealistic to rely on leaders who are also constrained by conventional politics, bounded rationality and the need to please their constituencies. The idea that some highly intelligent individual (hopefully benevolent, but maybe benevolence is prejudging the requirement) could somehow appear who could assess and analyse the global situation, decide, lead and implement a host of short, medium and long-term global actions, is an incredibly remote possibility. We would need one of the ten to the power three thousand genetic alternatives (see Chapter 2) to embody the genetic capability for delivering such skills (which in itself is highly unlikely) AND for that particular combination to be deployed within the next 10-20 years. Such a genetically-enhanced super person must have already been born.

History shows we have never had a globally acceptable or dominating leader. All leaders are transient and perforce must lead top-down anyway. A leader on his or her own is not, and could not be, a defining property of the human condition. But leaders are crucially important and given an idea on which they can build and lead may nonetheless have a considerable influence on how we evolve.

The hypothesis stands

So the hypothesis stands. As yet, there is no greater defining characteristic of the human condition so all encompassing and powerful as capitalism. The more than six billion people who currently occupy the Planet live in conditions which are almost exclusively determined by the capitalist system. A system in which the bankers can bring the UK to the edge of catastrophe, wreck numerous small businesses and still receive bonuses greater than the domestic product of some nations. Such is its power that the UK government, along with many other national governments, simultaneously provides the same banks with tax-payer-funded subsidies (see Chapter 1). Capitalism dominates government, it does not address poverty or hardship and because it inherently requires growth and consumption to succeed is, a priori, incompatible with a sustainable future for humankind. It must therefore be modified. What appears to be necessary, as this book endeavours to argue, is a political leader, or someone like Smith, Keynes or Friedman who had political influence, to break the mould and initiate the steps needed for a systemic change which aligns the self-interest of every individual with that of the world around him and her. What is required is a leader who can not only contemplate the *Big Society* but can understand and implement the systemic changes needed to bring it about.

Notes and references for chapter 4

4.1   *The oldest dated moon rocks have ages between 4.4 and 4.5 billion years and provide a minimum age for the formation of our nearest planetary neighbour. Thousands of meteorites, which are fragments of asteroids that fall to Earth, have been recovered. These primitive objects provide the best ages for the time of formation of the Solar System. There are more than 70 meteorites, of different types, whose ages have been measured using radiometric dating techniques. The results show that the meteorites, and therefore the Solar System, formed between 4.53 and 4.58 billion years ago.*
The best age for the Earth comes not from dating individual rocks but by considering the Earth and meteorites as part of the same evolving system in which the isotopic composition of lead, specifically the ratio of lead-207 to lead-206 changes over time owing to the decay of radioactive uranium-235 and uranium-238, respectively. Scientists have used this approach to determine the time required for the isotopes in the Earth's oldest lead ores, of which there are only a few, to evolve from its primordial composition, as measured in uranium-free phases of iron meteorites, to its compositions at the time these lead ores separated from their mantle reservoirs. These calculations result in an age for the Earth and meteorites, and hence the Solar System, of 4.54 billion years with an uncertainty of less than 1 percent. To be precise, this age represents the last time that lead isotopes were homogeneous throughout the inner Solar System and the time that lead and uranium was incorporated into the solid bodies of the Solar System. The age of 4.54 billion years found for the Solar System and Earth is consistent with current calculations of 11 to 13 billion years for the age of the Milky Way Galaxy (based on the stage of evolution of globular cluster stars) and the age of 10 to 15 billion years for the age of the Universe (based on the recession of distant galaxies).
Dalrymple, G. Brent, *The Age of the Earth,* Stanford University Press, 1994, ISBN-10: 0804723311, ISBN-13: 978-0804723312.

4.2   *Popper states that to be scientific a proposition must be capable of being exposed to experiments which might refute it. This definition humbles science since it doesn't claim absolute truth for science. Knowledge does not necessarily have to be scientific to be useful but if it claims to be scientific then it must be open to the possibility of being refuted by experiment or evidence. Thus Darwin's theory of evolution would be refuted for example, if we found fossil evidence that humankind were on the earth before the dinosaurs or it*

were shown that our methods of dating were wrong and the oldest date for the universe were say 6000 years ago rather than many billion.
Karl Popper, *Conjectures and Refutations,* Routledge and Kegan Hall, 1963, ISBN 0-415-04318-2

4.3 Herbert Simon, *Bounded Rationality and Organizational Learning, Organization Science , Volume 2, No.1, November ,1991.*

4.4 Herbert Simon, *Reason in Human Affairs", Stanford University Press, 1990, I*SBN-10: 0804718482, ISBN-13: 978-0804718486.

4.5 Paul Feyerband, *Science in a Free Society",* NLD London, 1987, ISBN 0 86091 753 3.

4.6 *New legislation by the UK Government from 1997 to 2008 contains 3,600 new laws – approximately one a day.*

4.7 *There are an estimated 4.2m CCTV cameras in the UK, or approximately one for every 15 people. Britain risks becoming an "Orwellian" society as CCTV cameras spread to quiet villages with low crime levels, a senior police officer warned yesterday. Ian Readhead, Hampshire's deputy chief constable, said he did not want to live in a country where every street corner was fitted with surveillance devices. He also criticised rules which meant DNA evidence and fingerprints could be kept for the rest of a teenager's life once they have been arrested for an offence, even if they never get in trouble again, and said there was a danger that speed cameras were seen by the public as a revenue-generating process rather than a genuine effort to reduce casualties.*
Mr Readhead highlighted the town of Stockbridge in Hampshire's rural Test Valley, where parish councillors spent £10,000 installing CCTV, as an example of a situation where the benefits of surveillance were questionable. Crime went up slightly in the town after the system was installed, Mr Readhead said, although between 2005 and 2006 there were only two violent crimes against people over 60 and no one was injured in either incident. "I have to question: does the camera actually instil in individuals a great feeling of safety and does it present serious offences taking place?" he said in an interview for the BBC's Politics Show.
"I'm struggling with seeing the deployment of cameras in our local village as being a benefit to policing; I understand why the local public say this is what we want, but I'm really concerned about what happens to the product of these

cameras, and what comes next? If it's in our villages - are we really moving towards an Orwellian situation with cameras on every street corner? I really don't think that's the kind of country that I want to live in."
Rachel Williams in the *The Guardian*, Monday 21ˢᵗ May, 2007.

4.8   Karl Popper, *The Open Society and Its Enemies,* Princeton University Press,1971, ISBN-10: 0691019681, ISBN-13: 978-0691019680.

4.9   Neil J. Cornish, David N. Spergel, Glenn D. Starkman and Eiichiro Komatsu, *Constraining the Topology of the Universe*, Physical Review Letters, Volume 92, No. 20, 21ˢᵗ May, 2004.

4.10   *"Because there is a law such as gravity, the universe can and will create itself from nothing. Spontaneous creation is the reason there is something rather than nothing, why the universe exists, why we exist. It is not necessary to invoke God to light the blue touch paper and set the universe going."*
Stephen Hawking and Leonard Mlodinow, *The Grand Design,* Bantam Books, 2010, ISBN 0553805371.

4.11   Richard Dawkins, *The God Delusion,* Mariner, 2006, ISBN-10: 0-618-91824-8, ISBN-13: 978-0-618-91824-0,

4.12   *On 3ʳᵈ November 2009 an appeal-court judge, Mr Justice Burton, overruled a previous ruling that had disallowed a claim for unfair dismissal by Mr Tim Nicholson. The earlier ruling held that because his views on environmental issues were scientific they were not covered by the existing laws which give employees with "philosophical or religious beliefs" the right to adhere to them in the course of their employment. The ruling brings scientific views into the realm of religion and philosophy.*

4.13   *While standing in for the regular biology teacher at Rhea County High School, Dayton, Tennessee, USA, the science teacher John Scopes assigned a chapter from G W Hunter's "Civic Biology" to his students to read. The chapter was about Darwin's theory of evolution. Scopes didn't deny that he had done this and declared he had taught some of the general points about evolution earlier the same month. As a result he was charged with teaching evolution in contradiction to the state law. The trial that followed became a contest between two great lawyers, William Jennings Bryan (prosecution) and Clarence Darrow (defence), and is famously called the Monkey Trial. Darrow,* *a leading lawyer with a national reputation, gave his time free because the issue was so important and aroused national interest. Scopes was convicted and fined $100. He was also offered free admission to a graduate programme at a leading university and became something of a celebrity.*

In 1962 a challenge to state anti-evolution law succeeded and the statute struck down as violating the United States' First Amendment's Establishment Clause.

On 26th September 2005 the Dover area school in Pennsylvania, USA, became a test case for deciding whether or not "intelligent creation"(also known as Intelligent Design or ID) should be taught alongside "evolution theory" as a valid alternative; the argument being that humans are so complex that some superior being must have designed us and we couldn't possibly have evolved. It is stated that statistically 45% of Americans believe humans were created in their present form by God and did not evolve. Fuel was earlier added to the controversy when President G W Bush declared that he personally felt that they should be taught together so that children are aware of the alternatives. While awaiting the court's judgment residents of the area voted off eight of the nine members of the school board responsible for bringing the action. The US District judge has since ruled that Intelligent Design (ID) is not science and rejected the action to make it so.

Meanwhile in November 2005, the Kansas Board of Education, Kansas, USA, approved new science standards for teachers in state schools that question Charles Darwin's teachings on evolution and handed a victory to advocates of intelligent design. The Board's 6-4 vote reverses a 2001 decision that affirmed Darwin's theory of natural selection. That vote came two years after most references to the theory were removed from state standards, making Kansas, according to one news report, the butt of jokes by scientists and late-night comedians.

This illustrates how traditions square up to each other to press their point of view. Are they seeking dominance or just the right to coexist? The issue is complicated because while many would not object to the two being taught separately as a religion and as science they seriously object to Intelligent Design being portrayed as a science. Many scientists have little problem in reconciling their religious beliefs with their scientific understanding and others protest that the separation of religion and state, which is written into the US constitution, should not be compromised. However, many ID people insist that ID is a science so no compromise is necessary.

The definition of science is possibly open to debate but Popper (1992), one of the most respected philosophers of the 20th century, has provided a widely accepted definition (See 4.2) which defines scientific knowledge as that which is open to experiments aimed at refuting that knowledge (theory or belief). So far Darwin's theory has not been refuted. In addition, ID is not capable of being exposed to refutation and while it may be respected as a religion, useful or helpful to many people who believe in it, it is not scientific, not part of science.

4.14   Thomas Kuhn, *The Structure of Scientific Revolutions,* The University of Chicago Press, (second edition), 1970, ISBN 0-226-45803-2

4.15   Bryan Magee, *The Great Philosophers,* Oxford University Press, 1983, ISBN 0-19-282201-2

4.16   Findlay, J. N., *Hegel: A Re-examination",* Oxford University Press, 1958, ISBN 0-19-519879-4.

4.17   *Lord (Alec) Broers is a leading engineer and was vice-chancellor of Cambridge University until 2003. He was chairman of the House of Lords committee on science and technology and president of the Royal Academy of Engineering when he delivered the 2005 Higher Education Policy Institute lecture at the Royal Institution in London.*
At this lecture he called for a broadening of degree courses and said that universities in Britain largely retained "the old model" of distinct faculties, homogenous courses and length of residence.
"Many new subjects have been introduced but the way they are arranged into silos and taught has remained largely unchanged for at least two centuries."
"I believe that what we need from our universities first and foremost is the provision for young people of an adequately broad knowledge base, together with modern analytical and communication skills. An undergraduate degree should cover the fundamentals of a coherent range of subjects. Too often, especially in science and engineering, students are fed indigestible quantities of pure mathematical background without its relevance being adequately explained. This merely leaves them in a state of confusion and disillusionment from which many never recover."
Lord Broers said those intending to specialise in law, medicine or other professions should follow their degree courses with two years of postgraduate study.
But schooling also needed to change.

"At present those going to our top universities are essentially required to decide whether they are going to pursue arts and humanities, or science and technologies, half way through their secondary schooling, The government's rejection of the Tomlinson proposals, which would have gone a long way to rectify this situation, was in my mind disastrous."

The problem stemmed largely from A-levels - "largely a 'memory' test", not sufficient in selecting students, which favoured the privileged because they depended heavily on the standard of teaching.

From a BBC report.

4.18 *A study of possible indoctrination and radicalisation of young people in India and Pakistan was made following the 9/11 attacks on the US. While religion forms a more significant component of education in these countries, the evidence is inconclusive that they produce a disproportionate number of terrorists (by western definition).While religion as the core of education may seem misdirected by western standards, it is simply accepted among Muslims in the East. A note posted by a young Muslim girl on the internet states, "I was learning The Holy Quran to understand Islam and striving to be a Hafiza (female who memorises the whole Quran) because I wanted to get enriched with all kinds of knowledge". She added that acquiring knowledge of any religion is a good practice.*

Saleem H. Ali, *Islam and Education: Conflict and Conformity in Pakistan's Madrassahs*, 2009, Oxford University Press, ISBN-10: 0195476727, ISBN-13: 9780195476729.

4.19 *"As in the political sphere, the child is taught that he is free, a democrat, with a free will and a free mind, lives in a free country, makes his own decisions. At the same time he is a prisoner of the assumptions and dogmas of his time, which he does not question, because he has never been told they exist. By the time a young person has reached the age when he has to choose (we still take it for granted that a choice is inevitable) between the arts and sciences, he often chooses the arts because he feels that here is humanity, freedom, choice. He does not know that he is already moulded by a system: he does not know that the choice itself is the result of a false dichotomy rooted in the heart of our culture. Those who do sense this, and don't wish to subject themselves to further moulding, tend to leave, in a half-unconscious, instinctive attempt to find work where they won't be divided against themselves. With all our institutions, from the police force to academia, from medicine to politics, we give little attention to the people who leave - that process of elimination which* *goes on all the time and which excludes, very early, those likely to be original and reforming, leaving those attracted to a thing because that is what they already like. A young policeman leaves the Force saying he doesn't like what he has to do. A young teacher leaves teaching, her ideas snubbed. This social mechanism goes almost unnoticed - yet it is as powerful as any in keeping our institutions rigid and oppressive.*

These children who have spent years inside the training system become critics and reviewers, and cannot give what the author, the artist, so foolishly looks for - imaginative and original judgment. What they can do, and what they do very well, is to tell the writer how the book or play accords with current patterns of feeling and thinking - the climate of opinion. They are like litmus paper. They are wind gauges - invaluable. They are the most sensitive of barometers of public opinion. You can see changes of mood and opinion here sooner than anywhere except in the political field - it is because these are people whose education has been just that - to look outside themselves for their opinions, to adapt themselves to authority figures, to 'received opinion' - a marvellously revealing phrase.

It may be that there is no other way of educating people. Possibly, but I don't believe it. In the meantime it would be a help at least to describe things properly, to call things by their right names. Ideally, what should be said to every child, repeatedly, throughout his or her school life is something like this: 'You are in the process of being indoctrinated. We have not yet evolved a system of education that is not a system of indoctrination. We are sorry but it is the best we can do. What you are being taught here is an amalgam of current prejudice and the choices of this particular culture. The slightest look at history will show how impermanent these must be. You are being taught by people who have been able to accommodate themselves to a regime laid down by their predecessors. It is a self perpetuating system. Those of you who are more robust and individual than others, will be encouraged to leave and find ways of educating yourself - educating your own judgment. Those that stay must remember, always and all the time, that they are being moulded and patterned to fit the narrow and particular needs of this particular society.'"

Doris Lessing, *The Golden Notebook*, Penguin, 1964, Grafton 1973 (reprinted 13 times), Paladin, 1989 (reprinted 3 times). ISBN 0 586 08923 3.

4.20   Karl Popper, *In Search of a Better World*, Routledge, 1992, ISBN 0-415-08774-0.

4.21   Jonathan Porritt, *Capitalism as if the World Matters,* Earthscan, 2005, ISBN-10: 1-84407-192-8, ISBN-13: 978-1-84407-192-0.

4.22   *The UK's Type 45 destroyer (also known as the D or Daring class) is an air defence destroyer of the Royal Navy which will replace its Type 42 destroyers. The first ship in the class, HMS Daring, was launched on 1ˢᵗ February, 2006 and commissioned on 23ʳᵈ July, 2009. In an "intensive attack" a single Type 45 could simultaneously track, engage and destroy more targets than five Type 42 destroyers operating together. The Daring class are the largest escorts ever built for the Royal Navy in terms of displacement. After Daring's launch former First Sea Lord, Admiral Sir Alan West stated that it would be the Royal Navy's most capable destroyer ever, as well as the world's best air-defence ship.*

Chapter 5
Complexity

"I am I plus my surroundings and if I do not preserve the latter I do not preserve myself."

José Ortega y Gassett (1883-1955)

Complexity illustrated through the identification of connections and the systemic relationship between the Planet and the human condition. The stakeholder model is derived and used to indicate the scope for a systemic change which includes the interests of the Planet itself.

Stakeholders

The *Big Society* is emerging in this book not so much as a vision of social science and a political idea of a young Prime Minister, but as an essential component of a world in which the self interest of individuals must be better aligned, through systemic change, with the interests of the Planet and the human condition in which they live. While alignment is definable, the form of the resulting socio-economic and political structures is uncertain for reasons of bounded rationality and its close cousin, complexity,

Complexity is much quoted in this book because intervening in complex systems has potentially unpredictable outcomes (see also Chaos Theory in Chapter 6). So far, of what exactly this complexity is comprised is unclear. This chapter thus illustrates complexity through a model based on connections and exchanges of value. The approach illustrates why the methods of government to govern by policies and fiscal control (i.e. the tools of capitalism) is inadequate and why a single, systemic change, applicable at the most elemental level at which human transactions occur, is likely to succeed. So how is the model devised?

There are literally thousands of diagrams, some might claim them to be models of organisation, proposed in both management and technical literature and almost anyone with an interest can come up with one. They are mostly prescriptive in that they describe how it should be done and follow the scientific tradition by mostly ignoring the variety in the human factor. Even the ubiquitous organisation chart fails to communicate the various character traits which actually determine who influences who. Few are models to fully represent what is being addressed, either in the sense of "model" as metaphor or in the sense of "model" illustrating an "ideal". Few justify the description "methodology", that is a method with a substantial body of knowledge and concepts to underpin and justify it. Most are just logical representations but from a limited view of a specific issue. In contrast, this chapter attempts to provide the means of addressing organisational issues holistically and tries to combine both science and the humanities in its approach.

It is not an easy task. Chapters 2, 3 and 4 have raised issues and stimulated ideas relevant to organisational evolution and global well being. But even the United Nations finds it difficult to tackle this (although hopefully they try) and for the average manager, student or ICT enthusiast it might seem unrealistically formidable. So where do we start? Whatever the answer, it has to be viable at the level of organisation and individual experience with which we are daily familiar. If a coherent framework is practical and credible at this level then it may also be practical and credible at other levels of aggregation; whether microscopic or macroscopic, at the subatomic level or the level of the cosmos. What we can at least try to do, is to develop a framework at a level with which we are familiar and simply ensure that it contains features which are plausible at other levels of aggregation and detail. We thus start with familiar things such as customers and employees. These latter two are clear examples of organisational stakeholders and a starting point for the framework at a work-a-day level of application.

A feature of stakeholders in modern commerce is that it is a widely accepted, and a mostly useful assumption, that by successfully meeting the expectations of that set of stakeholders we call customers, a trading company will meet the expectations of all other stakeholders. These include investors, employees, suppliers, law enforcers and government agencies. But this rather understates the size of the challenge and is a dangerous oversimplification. Information overload, uncertainties, rapid change, sustainability, finance, corporate social responsibility, government regulation, innovation and customisation have all to be managed simultaneously and well to compete. It is also an inadequate simplification when applied to public-sector organisations, especially in the case of the UK where approaching 50% of the economy is in the hands of the public sector. Here, councillors and the government itself are effectively surrogate stakeholders for both investors and customers. The assumption is fundamentally weak in that it takes no account of structural changes and organisational evolution such as the effect of deploying ICT (and other transforming technologies). It is also weak in regard to incorporating social mores and traditions, omits consideration of special interest groups and takes capitalism as a given.

The organisation illustrated schematically in Fig. 5.1 is the first step in creating the framework.. It recognizes from the outset that any organisation has many stakeholders. The particular set may vary from one organisation to another and the set in Fig. 5.1 is merely one example, typical of a manufacturing company. Manufacturing in the broadest sense is a particularly good example because it is reasonably generic. It encompasses marketing, selling, designing, procuring, controlling, employing, producing, distributing, subcontracting etc. It involves easy-to-imagine physical activities which help with explanations and it can be applied to most other organisations by simply adding or removing an appropriate stakeholder. If you understand the manufacturing organisation then understanding others should more easily follow, is the general idea.

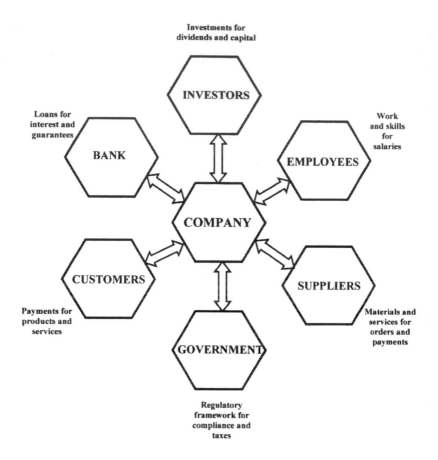

Figure 5.1 Stakeholders and their Expectations

Expectations

A few definitions are necessary to help explain the reasoning. So in Fig. 5.1 a stakeholder's expectations are met by means of a **transformation** carried out by a set of **activities**. The input to the transformation is pure expectation. The output is the meeting of the expectation. The actual or implied agreement by two stakeholders to engage in the transformation is a **transaction**. Thus I may go to the company which employs me with the expectation that after a month of responsible and satisfying effort, the

activity of working in the design office for example, I will receive a salary. The transaction is the exchange of my work for salary.

The transformation is the activities of me applying my skills at this place of work AND the company organising salary payment. In a similar way, investors who put loans or share capital at the disposal of a company do so with the expectation that they will receive shareholder dividends. The transaction is making the investment and receiving dividends. The transformation is the multiplicity of company activities which turn the investment into those dividends. Customers expect to receive products in return for paying the agreed price and suppliers expect payment for the goods they provide. The transaction is the customer handing over payment for goods or services received. The transformation is again the multiplicity of company activities which turn payment into goods or services.

An important conceptual point should be noted here. In all of the above, while money or physical goods may represent the satisfying of an expectation, the strict definition of output from the transformation is the satisfying (or possibly dissatisfying) of that expectation. Inputs to transformations are expectations. Outputs from them are satisfied or unsatisfied expectations. In the following development an input is NOT for example the supply of a raw material and the output is NOT a product for sale, although of course transformations of such things is the means by which expectations are defined. The things transformed, that is the stuff of which satisfied expectations are made, are here defined as **entities**. Money, pleasure, anger, energy, compensation etc. are all types of **entity.** What is, or is not, acceptable as an entity for the purposes of setting and meeting an expectation is largely determined by social and personal mores. Fig. 5.1 probably understates the relevant range of entities. Investors, for example, may invest because they feel pride in being associated with a particular company and many employees expect satisfaction as well as a salary.

Let us suppose I carry out work in the drawing office which meets the organisation's expectations of me. The organisation, for its part, carries out a series of **activities** which enables it to pay me and hence meet my expectations of it. There is a reciprocal relationship between us; we are each a stakeholder in the other. An organisation acting as a whole is, in fact, just another stakeholder.

One might recall Adam Smith's point here that self interest is a great motivator, or Karl Popper's that all creatures strive for a better life [4.20]. Satisfied expectations meet these criteria and as with exchanges of value, satisfaction of expectations should be reciprocated in any honest transaction.

Fig. 5.2 illustrates the point that the relationships illustrated in Fig. 5.1 are part of a network of interconnected stakeholders including ourselves. This network is so extensive as to be quasi-infinite for practical purposes. Away from my job I buy food from the supermarket and we, the supermarket and I, become mutually benefiting stakeholders. The supermarket buys food, delivered by vans, from farms, factories and similar suppliers. They in turn buy from others. The steak on my plate will have come via a series of inter-connected stakeholders and at some point it will have even belonged to a cow. Even this cow, could it express its view, might have to admit that its expectations of a well-fed, secure and even pampered life were met in return for it later becoming food. In turn the grass and other feedstuffs on which the cow fed can be regarded as stakeholders. And note that to be a stakeholder does not necessarily require consent; worms can expect to be eaten by birds and cows can expect to be eaten by many of us. So when we refer to stakeholders in a company we are really referring to the first line of stakeholders at the immediate boundary of that company.

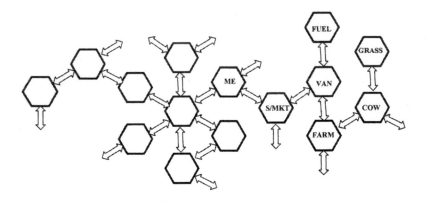

Fig 5.2 Stakeholders form a near Infinite Network

It may seem obvious that birds need to feed on worms and that I also need some to improve the soil in my garden. But there is no independent control over who gets how many worms. What we observe and get is the result of some complex dynamics. My garden doesn't normally have too many or too few worms and the birds mostly don't go hungry. This is not controlled of course, I am simply describing the current state of a continuously adjusting system which will always be explainable in systemic terms but not necessarily operating to our taste or benefit? I have sufficient worms in my garden because whatever I have is a fact of life to which I have always been accustomed. This self-adjusting equilibrium taking all possible interactions into account is the essence of Gaia theory. It is why top-down intervention often has unintended consequences. For example, a Government decree that we should increase the number of worms per garden could be enacted by reducing (killing) the number of birds which eat worms. But the decrease in birds would also increase insects, which might well reduce crop yields, which might make farming uncompetitive and increase imports and so on. This is true even before we consider the evolutionary process discussed in Chapter 2 whereby the combination of genes and alles may introduce a major change at any time.

In employment I also have a relationship with fellow workers. By providing my skills to the design office I simultaneously contribute to the company as a whole and must work to some kind of plan which ensures that whatever I do fits reasonably well with that of my colleagues. The design office functional group, including its equipment, is actually a stakeholder within the company. My expectations and those of the employer are actually satisfied (or not) through my contribution to the stakeholder "design office" and thence through the contribution of the design office to the company. The design office expects me and the rest of its stakeholders to do their jobs and the company expects the design office and other stakeholders within it, to do theirs. The network of interconnected stakeholders and the activities in which they engage to meet expectations thus extends both within and beyond the boundaries of any organisation. My kidneys similarly have a vested interest in me. They expect me to form suitable relationships with external stakeholders and my internal stakeholders - heart, mouth, stomach, lungs and so on - to do their bit.

Machinery, tools, computers, materials are all stakeholders. Just as grass may be a stakeholder in the world of a cow, a production machine can be a stakeholder in a company. The machine expects maintenance and fuel and the company expects it to operate to specification. These stakeholders are created deliberately or as a by-product of some more extensive process.

Of course as a business I may need some stakeholders such as banks, more than they need me in particular, although without a large number of people like me even banks would find life difficult. I am likely to be the beneficiary of others, such as suppliers and employees, and am able to choose between them and change allegiances from time to time. Yet some employees are so valuable I will do almost anything to retain them and some suppliers are unique! Also, a company may desperately need an investor but, once having got one, the investor may be unable to retrieve his investment and will be anxious for any kind of return rather than the total demise of the company holding his stake.

Connections are clearly very extensive. While simple to conceive as lines between stakeholders as in Fig. 5.2, it is very difficult to draw a diagram illustrating this point for more than a few. For those with a mathematical background the kinds of connection in Fig. 5.2 can be efficiently and more simply expressed as a matrix in which a 1 in a box indicates a **direct** transaction-based relationship and a zero no such (direct) relationship, as shown in Fig. 3.3 (a). Note that the diagonal is full of 1s thus indicating the relationship of a stakeholder with itself. Note also that the off-diagonal entries simply provide pairs which represent the same connection. Or mathematically, for a non-diagonal element in row x column y there is an identical element at row y and column x. If however the connections were replaced by the entities which are exchanged at each connection, one off diagonal (x, y) would be the entity received and the other off-diagonal (y, x) the entity delivered. This is illustrated in Fig. 5.3 (a) for just the pair of stakeholders, VAN and FUEL.

	GRASS	COW	FACTORY	VAN	FUEL	SUPER-MARKET	DESIGN OFFICE	ME	EMPLO-YER (MY)	FAMILY (MY)
GRASS	1	1								
COW	1	1	1							
FACTORY		1	1	1						
VAN			1	1	energy	1				
FUEL				money	1					
SUPER-MARKET				1		1				1
DESIGN OFFICE							1	1	1	1
ME								1		
EMPLO-YER (MY)							1	1	1	
FAMILY (MY)						1		1		1

(a) Connectivity at a given time T$_1$

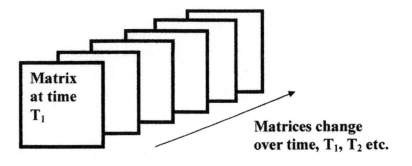

(b) Connectivity changing over time

Figure 5.3 Mathematical Representation of Stakeholder Connections

Very importantly we should also note that a particular matrix is only valid for a particular set of connections at a particular point in time, so in order to cover other possibilities Fig. 5.3 (a) should extend into the third dimension, with a new matrix being created at the time of any change in connectivity, as shown in Fig. 5.3 (b). While this may become too large for practical purposes it illustrates the concept.

Fig. 5.3 is arguably a fundamental expression of the connectivity of the "world" and illustrates a further important point. It shows me as a stakeholder not only as an individual but also as part of a stakeholder (design office) which is itself part of an organisation (employer). In fact most of us operate this way both satisfying our own needs and helping others to satisfy theirs. Thus in drawing Fig. 5.3 the "ME" actually occurs in several places. I am a stakeholder in my own right and also as a component in other stakeholders such as DESIGN OFFICE, MY FAMILY and MY EMPLOYER which employs me. Given that I in turn am made up of components - stakeholders at a lower level of microscopic detail - we can begin to form a theory and framework which is consistent at both the macroscopic and microscopic levels. These components/stakeholders of which I am comprised, such as blood, liver, bones and skin, might well consist of groupings of even lower-level stakeholders (atoms and molecules for example) and so on infinitesimally. As a flight of fancy, maybe that vital component in the human body which determines whether we are living or dead, is simultaneously present in all our body's stakeholders. It would explain why, when we die, everything dies at the same time and so completely. (The concept of the "soul" being a stakeholder is a novel idea, intended to offend no one.)

Processes

We may now examine the **connections** between stakeholders in more detail. Consider again my relationship with the company in which I work in the design office. At various places and times are a whole series of **activities** in which I have previously engaged which were necessary for me to meet the company's expectations. The act of me working in the design office is, among other factors, due to my education and training, my having breakfast that day, the supermarket providing porridge, my purchases of clothing and transport to the office among others. Another example is the surgeon who is only able to deliver his "services" by virtue of a similar process plus the processes by which the operating theatre came into being along with the team, the science underpinning the anaesthesia and drugs, the engineering which provides the replacement joints, sutures, monitors, scalpels, resuscitating equipment, probes, miniature cameras, X-ray, CAT and MRI scanners, kidney machines, and the rest.

My contribution to the company is only made possible by this prior set of activities which form an external process. And, for its part, the company meets my expectation of it by paying me a salary. This salary is derived from company **activities** provided by myself and many other internal stakeholder functions such as purchasing, sales, production and accounts.

Indeed, underpinning the contribution of every stakeholder is a sequence of activities which form a process. The investor must have learned his craft somewhere and succeeded in any number of deals to be in a position to invest. He or she will have also needed to eat, drink and dress in order to be what they are. Suppliers depend on large numbers of prior activities and customers will have needed to succeed in raising payment for goods ordered and so on. In fact many external activities contribute to processes prior to, currently with, or even after, the initial engagement between stakeholders e.g. education and lifestyle of an employee precedes contribution, customer and supplier negotiations are current, deliveries, after-sales service, payments and the handling of scrapped products occur later.

Everything is connected via processes and a change in one process has an effect on all others albeit the dilution may be so great as to be imperceptible to us in the majority of cases. The blowing up of an oilfield in Iraq may ultimately cause a fuel shortage, affect the response of an ambulance in Leeds and result in an "unnecessary" death. The loss of a replacement order for vehicles in Spain may cause the bankruptcy of a company in Birmingham and the subsequent breakdown of the marriage of its managing director. Things like this are of course happening all the time. In the majority of cases we do not know which everyday events we encounter are down to which events in what processes and where? Cause and effect in the wider environment of daily life are mostly related through very complex paths which are opaque to us individually.

All the above reinforces the reason for using "expectations" and "their satisfaction or not" as respectively inputs and outputs. It enables us to represent networks of stakeholder connections with all transformations being (a) generically of the same kind as in Figs. 5.2 and 5.3, and (b) open to human interpretation beyond the more limited and obvious description of the **entities** involved, including less tangible ones such as pleasure, anger, regret and security. The definition of inputs and outputs based on expectations means that any sequence of transformations making up a process is consistent although the entities involved may change. As an example, to supply me with a television requires a complex network of transformations involving entities such as information, capital, currency, materials and skills which are variously transformed separately and in combination at different stages in the process of providing me with what I expect. What I expect may also differ from what others who obtain televisions expect from the same physical transformation. For example the expectation might be "to be seen a good father", or "to keep up with the Jones' ", or to "keep the children quiet".

Stakeholder model of enterprise

Consider a single organisation such as a company, as shown in Fig. 5.1. This is a stakeholder and its internal activities and stakeholder network, however complex, may be viewed as a single activity for the purpose of its role in the wider network of stakeholders. This **activity** carries out (or fails to carry out as is occasionally the case) the set of transformations needed to meet its external stakeholder expectations. What I do is to carry out my work in the design office, a contributory part of the company's **activity**. The result is a mutually beneficial reciprocal **transformation,** "work for pay" and "pay for work (skills etc.)". The **transformation** links the process represented by the sequence of **transformations** which led to my being skilled and fit enough to do the work. There are of course corresponding processes by which each of the other external stakeholders in the company must have been involved in order to be one of its stakeholders.

At first sight it appears money flows in one direction and other entities in the other but this is not generally true. More profoundly other entities may flow in either or both directions and be positive or negative (dissatisfaction being the negative of satisfaction). There may even be more than one entity in either direction.

If a celebrity buys a house in Hollywood the obvious transformation is money for a house. But in addition Hollywood residency conveys additional status on the celebrity who may thence claim "to have arrived". Hollywood property prices rise (or fall as appropriate to the celebrity's status) and real estate agents benefit (or not). Entities such as a gain in status by the purchaser and improved business prospects for the real estate agent are not money. If my grandson joins his local football club, he gets the benefit of playing for a prestigious team and they get his football skills (a positive contribution to the team and an arrangement which deprives any opposition of his services). Prestige and skills are not money.

For the moment, if we continue with the company we arrive at Fig. 5.4, which is derived from the explanations represented by Figs. 5.1, 5.2 and 5.3. It illustrates a generalised form of organisation called the stakeholder-model of enterprise. The table in which each activity is labelled is part of the model since the lines which border each "box" represent an interface at which a transaction is defined and the box contains some activity which carries out the appropriate transformation(s). External stakeholders are shown along one axis and the internal stakeholders (functional activities) along the other.

	Marketing	Sales	Design	Procurement	Production	Delivery	Accounting	
Customers								Payments for products and services
Suppliers								Goods for payment
Employees								Work for salaries and satisfaction
Investors								Investment for dividends and capital
Banks								Loans for interest payments
Government								Regulations for taxes
Planet								**Something for nothing !**

Figure 5.4 Stakeholder Model of Enterprise

The model can be applied to any organisation by simply designating the appropriate external and internal stakeholders and transformations.

The stakeholder model is that of an organised activity (set of complex, internally connected stakeholders and activities in practice) which carries out transformations to meet the mutually beneficial expectations of itself and its external stakeholders who, in doing so, make the organisation itself a stakeholder. The transformations variously assemble, dissemble and redistribute the entities which represent stakeholder expectations into entities representing the satisfaction (or otherwise) of those expectations. These entities derive from a small generic set which apply in part or in whole to all transformations and are constrained by the environment in which the organisation operates.

We may summarise this by way of definitions:

- Stakeholders are groups or individuals, including inanimate objects, which engage with each other in an activity to meet mutually compatible expectations. This is what makes them stakeholders in each other and defines what is meant by stakeholder.

- The meeting of mutually compatible expectations is called a transformation and results in a two-way exchange of entities between stakeholders.
- What are acceptable as entities are determined by the needs and traditions which make up the environment in which the stakeholders operate.
- Stakeholders form networks in which expectations, satisfied or not, flow in both directions represented by entities which themselves may differ from one node in the network to the next (not just money).
- We are all stakeholders in our own right but may also have a separate role, internally, in any number of other organisations or groups which are themselves stakeholders, including those with which we have a stakeholder relationship such as a family, team or employing organisation.
- In a stakeholder network an organisation may be viewed as carrying out a single activity at just one node.
- Networks of stakeholders and the associated transformations form processes
- The stakeholder-model of enterprise represents the relationship between internal stakeholders (e.g. individuals, functional areas or teams) and transformations which meet the expectations of the external stakeholders. This latter point has a bearing on Business Process Re-engineering (BPR). Exponents of BPR have argued for some years about the number of fundamental processes an organisation has or should address. Stakeholders clearly define the major processes albeit that the task of management is to prioritise and manage the internal transformations required to nurture and control them.

Implications

The systemic approach has illustrated the interdependence of everything which occurs on the Planet Earth. It does not explain how each element functions but proffers insights into the overall connectivity and insofar as each element is made up of sub-elements is a new way of looking at things. This is consistent with the changing paradigm of science discussed in the next chapter. Traditional science looks at the bits and was forever seeking the smallest. New science is holistic and recognises the challenges of connectivity, complexity and chaos.

In particular we are now able to:
- Identify processes, that is sequences of transactions through which entities are exchanged and make the range of entities which can be transacted more explicit.
- Appreciate that value is accumulated by processes, that any one transaction depends on a history of previous transactions and hence a multiplicity of exchanges of entities. My contribution to the design office is not due to me alone; the surgeon is only one of many who make a surgical operation possible. An investor is only one player in a company's performance.
- Identify the contribution of non-animate and non-human stakeholders to processes i.e. the contribution of the Planet in a multiplicity of ways.
- Realise the inadequacy of top-down policies in achieving predictable outcomes because the connections are so complex.
- Identify where an intervention might be made to influence the exchange of value i.e. at the level of transactions.
- Demonstrate that those things which are derived from the Planet are not included in the capitalist system since the entity "money" does not pass to the Planet in any transaction in which the Planet is a stakeholder.

The concept of stakeholders and the stakeholder model of enterprise opens a whole new subject area beyond the aims of this book which affects business development and management. It relates directly to Porter's ideas on the value chain which emphasises the need to streamline those internal processes which add value and eliminate those which do not [3.29]. It refines and extends business process re-engineering [3.30, 3.31] about which there has been much discussion and little agreement on how many processes an organisation should address. Competitive businesses do not operate in either functional silos or process tunnels. Clearly one is not an alternative nor a remedy for the other. Success is much more likely when functions and processes operate in sympathy; a challenge for modern managers and at a national level, for politicians too.

Conclusions

The combination of Fig. 5.3 and the above explanatory text is succinct and encapsulates both the constituent components of the Planet and the Planet as a whole. At the same time it illustrates the sheer complexity of the Planet Since the Planet and ourselves are developing to yet greater complexity we should take steps to ensure we evolve sustainably. We should pay attention to the insights of Simon on bounded rationality and the lessons of chaos theory and the law of unintended consequences. We should reflect on Koestler's point that higher forms (of life) display more complexity than lower forms and that according to Ashby's Law, we therefore need systems which have a comparable number of degrees of freedom to manage that complexity.

Stumbling block number one is that the Planet is a serious stakeholder in human affairs but not effectively represented in the capitalist system. But it is clearly a party to many transactions and extensively involved. The stakeholder approach offers hope. It indicates the practicality of intervening at the transaction level by simply assigning value to the Planet and recognizing its de-facto presence as a stakeholder. At a stroke its interests would then be represented. The mechanism is simple. The Planet could charge for what is consumed by others and pay for anything of value that it can buy back.

This representation of the Planet in the capitalist system reinforces what Ashby says about adding attributes to a system to cope with an increase in the variety of the environment. The global population, its activities and connections have so increased that humankind must itself assume a higher form; capitalism must evolve to cope with the increasing complexity and bring a consideration of the Planet's interests into the decisions of every citizen.

This reasoning is consistent with Simon's concept of bounded rationality. We are unlikely ever to understand the whole of humankind and its relationship with the Planet – the foregoing stakeholder model alone should reinforce the observation of just how complex it actually is – but we can make an intervention which rectifies the omission. We can make a change to our niche so that environmental sustainability is universally taken into account at the level of individuals, independent of political policy and just a systemic fact. The outcome, whatever it might be, should thence be more favourable to our survival than the current capitalist niche which neglects it.

To reinforce the message in this book, the stakeholders FUEL and GRASS in Fig. 5.3 (a) are part of a process which starts with the Planet (i.e. oil, seeds and chemicals in the soil). The Planet is clearly a stakeholder but the exchange of entities is unequal. What does the Planet now get in exchange for its oil and chemicals? Nothing!

Chapter 6
Technology

"Not what I have, but what I do is my kingdom" Thomas Carlyle
(1795-1881)

*"And we must proclaim science both as an intellectual challenge
and as a prerequisite for meeting humanitarian imperatives - health,
education and 'clean energy' for the developing world"* Professor Martin
Rees, Reith Lectures, 2010

**Technology is a major component of evolutionary change but
what do we mean when we refer to technology? How does technology
figure within our educational system and can we trust it? What is
the underlying cause of environmental change and could technology
provide a solution?**

Definitions

It was stated in Chapter 1, that science, engineering and technology
would be used with more or less the same meaning. This is because of
common usage and the seemingly general desire of the media to avoid
sorting out the finer distinctions. They use the terms science, technology
and occasionally engineering more or less interchangeably. Or as the joke
goes among engineers, when there is a success it is always scientists who
achieved it, when there is a failure it is down to the engineers!

In addition, science, engineering and technology are often abbreviated
in the UK to SET (sometimes STEM to include mathematics) and these
acronyms are widely used in schools to define a range of career options.
But acronyms are hardly the best way to communicate and using all
three terms is confusing and wearing for the reader. Thus with the caveat
that there is an important distinction of purpose between science and

engineering the term "technology" is often used here as a collective noun for all three. But it is worth looking at each in more detail because the distinctions are philosophically very important. A deeper understanding of what technology, science and engineering are all about can be gleaned from an insight of Emmanuel Kant [6.1] which is especially relevant at the point where evolution, technology and faith intersect.

Kant is universally recognised as one of the world's great philosophers. He postulated that the world we live in and observe is only part of another world of which we have no knowledge or experience. This larger world he called the world as it is in itself. Most engineers and scientists would delight in his reasoning, that the world as it appears to us ($W_{\text{as it appears to us}}$) is not determined solely by the world as it is in itself ($W_{\text{as it is in itself}}$), as it really is, but is limited by the sensors with which we experience and perceive it. Such sensors are not just the five obvious ones but include all human understanding, especially that which derives from scientific measurements and theories to probe and explain what is around us. The $W_{\text{as it appears to us}}$ is the world we unthinkingly and commonly refer to simply as the world. But according to Kant, the $W_{\text{as it appears to us}}$ is only part of the $W_{\text{as it is in itself}}$. The $W_{\text{as it is in itself}}$ is, in its totality, "unknowable" and although some people attribute properties to the unknowable part, such attributes and beliefs are pure faith and not part of science and engineering. This separation is a great help because scientists and engineers of all faiths, including atheists and agnostics, can in principle agree on scientific knowledge while disagreeing on matters of faith It is an elegant explanation of how technology and religious beliefs can coexist and, since Kant died more than 200 years ago, surprisingly little known or discussed today.

Of course there are some dissenters of whom the intelligent design and creationist communities, particularly but not exclusively in the USA, are current examples. They claim as scientific knowledge things which are matters of faith. Their prime example is that the world (and they do not distinguish the known and unknowable worlds) was created in seven days. To maintain this latter claim they have to refute the definition of scientific knowledge which is generally accepted by the vast majority of scientists and engineers and is elegantly expressed by Karl Popper [6.2].

My personal belief is that there may or may not be a $W_{\text{as it is in itself}}$ which is greater than, and inclusive of, the $W_{\text{as it appears to us}}$. My belief is that I should be open minded to the possibility of that wider world and should admit that I am ignorant of it. It may or may not be greater than the world we have so far identified through science and our personal senses. But what we have already sensed as the $W_{as\ it\ appears\ to\ us}$, is in itself a marvel, an amazing phenomenon in which we and the planet Earth are so small that one might reasonably conclude we are insignificant. The words in the song from the film, "The Meaning of Life", provide an elegant, amusing and technically accurate summary of what may be found in any serious book on astronomy [6.3]. The overwhelming experience of delving into what we know of this $W_{as\ it\ appears\ to\ us}$ is one which our increasing awareness of the scale of things merely adds to the awe in which we come to regard it. For example the Earth is in a galaxy we call the Milky Way which is more than 100,000 light years wide, within a Universe 156 billion light years wide and only one of many billions of galaxies each containing billions of stars.

Engineers and scientists generally share the above beliefs but differ in their complementary roles. Science in its purest form is concerned with understanding the $W_{as\ it\ appears\ to\ us}$. It is about improving our knowledge of it through experiment and the devising testable hypotheses about its physical and organic complexity. Science is not about the $W_{as\ it\ is\ in\ itself}$ which may or may not be limited to the world they seek to understand through nuclear physics and astronomy. Belief in it being greater than the $W_{as\ it\ appears\ to\ us}$, is of course a matter of faith. Some are religious and believe in a particular explanation, such as Christianity or Judaism, and an almighty God. Some are agnostic and believe there is something other than a God but do not feel able to define it. Atheists believe there is nothing.

For a definition of engineering it is helpful to turn again to Popper. He believed that evolution is driven at all levels by a desire to solve problems in pursuit of a better life. Thus engineering, in contrast to science, is about human-problem solving and that search for a better life. It requires an understanding of the products and the tools of science but its purpose is the synthesis of solutions to life's problems and the seeking out of life-enhancing opportunities. Its tools are not limited solely to those of science and it may sometimes use those of social science, for example as a concern in design, when explaining opportunities, introducing new technologies or examining ethical issues. (I will not enter the debate of whether social science is indeed a science – it plausibly claims scientific methods although its knowledge, while often useful, is not strictly scientific.)

Engineering and science are complementary processes which have a significant influence on human evolution as shown in Figure 6.1. The science-focused process is concerned with understanding the $W_{as\ it\ appears\ to\ us}$ which changes continuously, partly as a result of the engineering-focused process of solving problems. The engineering process is a concern for where we go and what could be. The $W_{\text{as it appears to us}}$ is not stagnant and we need to continually address problems and articulate our understanding of them (science) ahead of creating solutions and implementing them (engineering).

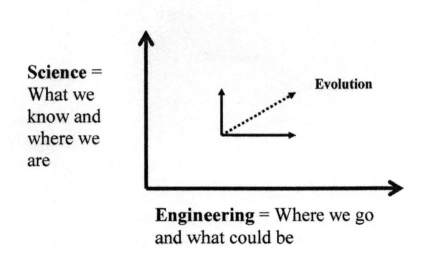

Figure 6.1 Complementary Nature of Engineering and Science

Probably the best, most recent and alarming example of these complementary processes is part of the reason for this book (addressing climate change). It is the discovery through science of the link between man-made components of the $W_{\text{as it appears to us}}$ and adverse climate change [6.4]. Without doubt the solutions are through engineering which is determining, and will determine, the many environmentally sustainable alternatives of where we might go and the world as it could be ($W_{\text{as it could be}}$).

Unfortunately there are obstacles as shown in Figure 6.2. Engineering is not only constrained by science but by social, political and economic factors. **By far the most constraining is the economic factor; the criterion of capitalism that the markets should decide.**

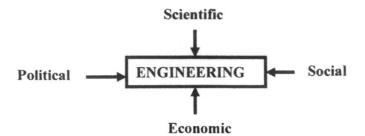

Figure 6.2 Constraints on Engineering

So we have definitions for science and engineering, what about technology? For those who would like a more rigorous definition of technology per se, I suggest, **"the manifestation of artefacts and processes which are encountered in science and engineering but which has no intellectual or philosophical significance other than by association with those two"**. More generally and simply, the word "technology" appears to be useful as a generic term for all new ideas which are not readily understood or even explicable to the average citizen.

And what of medicine, isn't that the application of science? Well, yes. It's comprised of activities which are directly analogous to engineering and is philosophically identical. Medics might claim some special uniqueness because of "their commitment to human life". But, bearing in mind Popper's definition of evolution, it is difficult to agree their claim. Isn't that what engineering is all about – improving the human condition? This would seem to be the case both generally and in detail, since many advances in medicine are due to science and engineering, from X-ray machines to key-hole surgery, prosthetics, dialysis, replacement joints and artificial hearts, the MRI scanner, ultrasound and a plethora of drugs, monitoring equipment and technologically enabled techniques. Perhaps the most important contribution of all was Faraday's discovery and work on electromagnetic induction which made electricity possible. Imagine hospitals without electricity.

Two cultures

An additional feature of technology is the relationship between those who understand it and those who don't. It is now more than 50 years since C P Snow gave his famous Rede lecture to a Cambridge audience in which he launched the phrase "the two cultures" [6.5]. This remains with us today as a shorthand for what he went on to describe and analyse as the divide between "literary intellectuals" and "natural scientists". This divide, which appears to be particularly prevalent in the UK, has led to mutual incomprehension and suspicion. Worse still, it is probable as Snow claimed, that it has had damaging consequences for the prospects of applying technology to the alleviation of the world's problems.

The split remains. There is the culture of technology on the one hand, and that of the arts and humanities on the other. My own school education culminated in a choice between the science sixth or the arts sixth (corresponding to ages 16-18 for most children) which led to the almost complete separation of the vocational aspiration and intellectual development of the two cohorts. Much of this was due to the circumstance of separation rather than any fundamental differences in ability. I distinctly recall grappling with the mysteries of differential equations while an "arts" colleague, who I happened to meet on the playing field, was reading Machiavelli's "The Prince" [6.6]. It wasn't until my 40's that I discovered the relevance of the latter to the strategic issues I needed to confront in my business at that time. It was also a revelation to me that Machiavelli's writing is not one of evil intent and wickedness as I had, in my semi-educated way, been led to assume previously. "The Prince" is actually an easy-to-read, common-sense treatise on how and why nation states actually operate and survive. It may appear shocking because it is not how we would ideally like them to operate, but undoubtedly explains what in our hearts we acknowledge and even accept in reality. As with much common sense it is only common when someone such as Machiavelli, points it out. My life would have been richer, maybe in the material as well as spiritual sense, had "The Prince" been a sixth-form rather than a middle-age experience.

One of the most unjust and irrational consequences of the cultural divide is the widespread belief that engineering in particular is not creative and is boring. This stems in part from the use of the term "creative arts" which is too easily misconstrued to imply that other subjects are not creative. However, a hypothetical observer visiting the Planet a 100 years ago and then again now, will clearly witness the technological differences **created** in the intervening period and its effects in reducing drudgery, generating wealth, providing entertainment and inspiring leisure. Technology is exciting not boring to most of those who understand it. A non-scientifically-educated person is bound to feel bored and excluded when they are unable to contribute meaningfully to any serious technical discussion. As an Electrical Engineer, the content of my two engineering degrees required, and most of my technical work requires, mathematical and geometric models (or practical metaphors if you prefer) to express and examine the unseen and unseeable phenomenon we call electricity. Fellow professionals share them as a kind of language although they are more than that because they are able to encompass physical laws, hypotheses, designs and theories too. The amazing and truly creative ideas which emerge from practitioners in the field are expressed in such terms and are opaque to those who do not understand them.

One example is the innovative work of Gabriel Kron [6.7]. He developed an elegant method of analysis in electrical engineering by defining the electromagnet and electrostatic interactions which are fundamental to the operation of electrical machines and circuits in a very simple form and quite separately from the way they bear on particular applications. He thence showed that a particular application could be defined specifically by a "connection" matrix comprised of "ones" and "zeros". The combination of his generalised form of the physical laws with the appropriate matrix then defined the application. This is partly my inspiration for the analysis of Chapter 5 wherein I suggest that a connection matrix defines the human condition and its relationship with the Planet. If we only knew what the fundamental component of the relevant physical laws might be, such as an understanding of our world at an elemental level, then the matrix might well provide a link between the macroscopic and microscopic approaches which science still strives to discover.

Another is the content and control of any major electricity generating system; taken for granted because non-technically-educated people do not begin to understand the essence of the achievements nor the issues and problems overcome. Much of this is also true of modern communications systems, the internet, virtual reality, avatars, iPods and 3-D television.

The above and the beauty of the Mandelbrot Set, a purely mathematical creation as explained below, surely surpass what pass for modern art such as the unmade bed with unwashed knickers or half a sheep in formaldehyde by creative artists Tracy Emin [6.8] and Damien Hirst [6.9] respectively?

We can express the weaknesses of the above in Kantian terms. The $W_{\text{as it appears to an individual from the humanities}}$ and the $W_{\text{as it appears to a technologist}}$ are both small, incomplete and different subsets of the $W_{\text{as it appears to us}}$; that is the world in which "us" is the corporate "us" and represents the whole of what humankind knows. But for reasons of evolutionary variety (we are each unique even within our species), bounded rationality and differences in real-life experiences, the $W_{\text{as it appears to us}}$ is already limited and different for every individual. To this gigantic mix of world views we then provide a system of education which reduces commonality of understanding of the $W_{\text{as it appears to us}}$. This is a recipe at government level for conflict, fear of the unknown, ill-conceived policies and indecision. Take just the one example of Ashby's Law of Requisite Variety (see Chapter 2). The concept originated in the highly mathematical world of cybernetics yet has, as this book explains, a massive bearing on the human condition and provides a powerful tool to decide what is and what isn't possible.

There is of course a much more diverse choice of subjects to be learned by young people today, but competition for places at the best universities and in demanding subjects such as science, engineering, modern languages and medicine, continues to force specialisation at an early age. Universities do offer courses which allow students to obtain a degree by studying a wide range of modules but again the more demanding subjects require the cumulative development of skills and understanding. This means that year three of a degree subject is impractical without previously studying foundation material in years one and two successfully. It means that a school-leaver must already have studied to reach an acceptable level of skill to be able to even enter a specialist undergraduate course. The mathematical tools required of a top engineer are typically acquired over seven years of secondary education and two to four years of undergraduate study.

Such is the rate at which new knowledge is emerging that science, engineering and technology subjects have many more options to cover and offer. For example, due to the explosion in materials, bio-, nano- and semi-conductor technology, electronics, automatic control and communication systems, it now requires around 40 staff to cover the undergraduate specialisms in electrical engineering alone when only eight were needed 25 years ago. Computing is a mainstream, essential subject now while just a generation ago it was only the peripheral choice of a minority. Yet, students still have only three or four years available to obtain a first degree. While the freedom to choose options outside their root culture may be desirable and in theory easier, the number, desirability and attractiveness of options within the root culture have increased too.

The result is a steady stream of partially educated individuals. Many leave university with only a superficial understanding of the breadth of knowledge which characterises the totality of human endeavour and are unaware of the limitations of themselves or the narrow culture they have experienced. Witness major mistakes such as the commissioning of London Airport's Terminal 5 [6.10], the sheer innumeracy of the UK tax adjustments in 2008 and 2010 [6.11] and the limited vision referred to by Professor Brian Cox in regard to the wonders of the Universe [6.12]. Two recent Prime Ministers, Tony Blair and Gordon Brown are both arts graduates. Blair is lawyer and self-confessed technophobe [6.13]. Brown has a PhD in history. During their period in charge of the UK Government, the gap between the rich and the poor widened, manufacturing declined and we budgeted to spend more than we earned.

The explanation of how the gap widens is simple arithmetic and predictable. Assume two people are earning respectively £10,000 a year and £100,000 a year and that each receives an annual rise of 2% in line with inflation (the usual criterion). Their new earnings become £10,200 and £102,000 respectively and the gap widens from £90,000 to £91,800. Over ten years of this typical rate of inflation, the higher earner will come to receive an income which has increased by more than the lower paid even earns.

The results are an increasing sense of unfairness and severe economic difficulty. It is difficult not to conclude that they, Brown and Blair, were mostly unaware of what, according to Plato, the Oracle at Delphi said "That the wisest of men is the one who, like Socrates, recognises that in reality he is not wise".

Changing paradigms

During the late 20th century there was a revolution in scientific thinking due to the emergence of complexity as a serious subject for scientific research. Complexity derives from Chaos theory which is attributed to Lorenz, a professor of meteorology at MIT nicknamed the father of Chaos theory. There are now many books on this subject by a wide range of respected scientists [6.14, 6.15, 6.16]. The principal feature of Chaos theory is the discovery that, in the calculation of the solution for some problems, it is possible to obtain very different answers for quite minute changes in the values entered as a starting point. Hitherto, a small change or error in a starting value was thought to lead to a small change in the solution which would still be recognisable as essentially the same. However computers have provided the means of solving ever-more complicated problems, for which the solutions may be genuinely defined by a set of equations, with data which can be expressed to minute levels of accuracy. Thus it is possible to use numbers which are accurate to tens of decimal places and to alter them by as little as one significant digit, thereby revealing the phenomenon. It is not that the equations are wrong, it is that they are right and the sensitivity to small changes is genuine.

The kinds of problems which exhibit chaos are often everyday things like forecasting the weather. The physics of the way the weather is formed and changes over time is describable by non-linear equations (relationships) and it is now known that it is the non-linearity which causes the chaotic phenomena. Cloud formations and the waves on the sea are examples of chaos in practice, demonstrating that it is not just in the physical representation and calculation that chaos arises, but that it is an intrinsic feature of clouds and waves. There are many examples because in real life non-linear relationships (equations) are more usual than linear ones.

French mathematician Benoit Mandelbrot has demonstrated complexity in his summations of various non-linear mathematical series, the solutions to which can be calculated and thence plotted in two dimensions. Numerous images of "Mandelbrot" sets, [6.17] many calculated by others using high-precision computers, are available over the internet. An example is shown in Figure 6.3. The solutions here are defined according to whether or not a mathematically defined series converges when the complex number represented by the coordinates at a point in the diagram is inserted into that series. If it does then a (small) dot is printed. The colour of the dot may be coded according to how rapidly the calculation converges to a solution to provide amazingly intricate patterns.

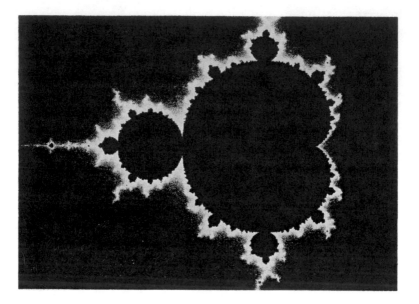

Figure 6.3 The Mandelbrot Set

Amazingly, if the values of the coordinates are progressively varied by minute values around any given point, the dots continue to form patterns, regardless of how small the changes in value might be. The patterns change and to a significant degree seem to repeat as shown. This nesting of images is an example of a solution to non-linear equations giving widely differing results for very small changes in the initial values i.e. dot or no dot, a pretty large difference in outcome!

So in one sense our understanding of the world about us has taken a step forward. But, possibly more significantly, it has also revealed our own ignorance in an area we had not expected. While we already knew the world to be complex we had nonetheless underestimated just how complex that might be. We now have reason to question our philosophy and technology is grappling with a whole range of ideas in which complexity and chaotic phenomena appear centre stage. "Understanding the whole" has joined "an understanding of the parts" as a respectable component in the philosophy and advancement of science.

This is exactly what Kuhn predicted in his seminal book on the nature of scientific revolutions [4.14]. For many of the past 200 years or so, science was concerned to identify the most basic unit of matter – the elementary particle. The idea being that if we knew what the most basic building block of our world might be then we might then (easily?) predict how combinations of it would behave and hence obtain the key to the universe. For example, as a schoolboy in the middle of the 20th century, I was taught unambiguously that the atom was the smallest constituent of matter. But, the splitting of the atom, the nuclear bomb and the experimental results from several particle accelerators meanwhile, have demonstrated that this is not the case. The issue of what constitutes the basic building block of matter is now bound up in ideas such as string theory and its concept of 22 dimensions [6.18].

A second less heralded change of paradigm has been discerned by Mike Gibbons and his team [6.19]. They define two types of knowledge, Mode 1 and Mode 2. Mode 1 is essentially the formal, structured knowledge we learn from textbooks and lectures. Mode 2 is the experiential kind which relates to context, experience and ongoing, individual and corporate learning. It is an almost ephemeral form of knowledge possessed by a company or group and held collectively. It is the knowledge of how things are done, what succeeds and what doesn't, how to deal with this and how to avoid that. It is evolutionary in that when decisions are made which have a bad effect, understanding is improved. If a decision has a good effect an understanding is reinforced. Mode 2 knowledge is dynamic and tacit rather than formal. It is sometimes learned by accident rather than design, implicit not explicit.

A much greater awareness of the value of Mode 2 knowledge and how to manage and husband it would seem to be long overdue. While Mode 1 knowledge can be copied relatively easily or stolen through industrial espionage, Mode 2 is an elusive, multi-cephalous, corporate kind of thing, difficult to identify. In the significant matter of international competition, Mode 2 knowledge is of considerable value.

Technology, democracy and capitalism

In the developed world, technology is so taken-for-granted that it assumes, and is assumed to be, an unquestioned feature of life. The culture characterised by a take-technology-for-granted society is so great a part of what is accepted as normal that it may be even be undermining democracy itself. It is so advanced in relation to what is understood or understandable by lay people, even the allegedly educated, that decisions about how we deploy it often confound or lie outside the democratic process. For example in the UK, the public fear of anything nuclear and of anything likely to change the countryside, such as wind turbines, makes it very difficult to have a reasoned debate about measures to ameliorate the projected effects of climate change. Self-interest and not-in-my-backyard attitudes compound the problem. Meanwhile energy-wasteful, emissions-producing transport and inadequate housing stock continue to damage the environment. The Government hesitates; it is afraid to make planet-saving decisions on these matters because it might lose votes.

Meanwhile those familiar with technology are unable to communicate effectively because their explanations are too complex and discussions are reduced to uninformed, emotionally-driven contests. And since technology does not by its nature compete with emotional and political argument, it simply proceeds inexorably where it can in the markets where the demonstration of economic success wins nearly every time. Anything which is within the law and makes money is "alright" (and even the law is often no impediment as with drug abuse and corporate corruption).

In this way, new technology does not enter the public's consciousness until it is having an effect, so debate tends to follows rather than precede its implications. As a democracy we find it difficult to make major policy decisions about technological matters and fail to set policies which moderate the many small technical decisions and then accumulate to largely define our society. Warm houses, rapid transport, easy-to-maintain clothes, labour-saving machinery, on-line education courses, television and films, countless forms of entertainment, electricity, sewers and clean water, antibiotics, palliative medicines and keyhole surgery are perceived as good but other examples less obviously so. Excessive and unnecessary waste, indestructible plastic and litter, oversized cars, congested roads, polluting aircraft, addictive and oversweet food, obesity, diabetes and health-service costs to remedy self-induced ills, the misuse of entertainment technologies and widespread preoccupation with talent-less celebrities and poor role models, high-density recording media and addiction to video games, internet chat rooms and the seduction of children, medical advances and the moral uncertainties which surround the artificial prolonging of life, thalidomide, cosmetic surgery and performance enhancing drugs for cheating athletes and so on. Democratically we might approve of some of these but it is doubtful. The point is that they arrived, driven by the pursuit of money without prior understanding or democratic approval.

The effect of technology on human evolution is thus self-evidently massive. Its dominance of human affairs, especially in the 19th, 20th and 21st centuries is breathtaking. Homo sapiens is the only animal to harness the two things which are most responsible for the incredible success of its species. They are the understanding and control of energy and the development of global communications. The control of energy has released humans from the full-time work of merely surviving and given them the time to think, solve problems and seemingly improve their lot. Global communications have facilitated education, the spread of ideas, solutions to problems, the use of money as a system of exchange, the influence of leaders and many processes of collaboration. Yet human activity still remains subordinate to the constraints of the capitalist system.

Environmental sustainability

To find a solution to the problem of environmental sustainability we need to understand the principal features of our environment. The starting point is (a) that without the Sun we would not exist since all life on earth owes its continuing existence to the energy we receive from the Sun, and (b) that consistent with the laws of thermodynamics, energy cannot be created or destroyed but merely changed from one form to another.

The mechanisms by which energy from the Sun is turned into heat and thence radiated into space can easily be explained. Energy entering the Planet's atmosphere is initially absorbed in a variety of ways, ranging from the chemical processes which help crops and vegetation to grow, to the animal life which eats them (including ourselves) to provide its energy and growth. It also creates the weather because the Earth rotates on its own axis and the Sun's energy is received by those parts which are in daylight and lost to space from those which are in night. The changes in air temperature cause pressure differences around the globe and hence winds. The temperature differences also change the amount of moisture taken up by the atmosphere. When a cloud cools we get rain and sometimes snow. Whatever happens to the energy from the sun it eventually becomes heat. If for example I cut down a tree and burn it, the burning releases the energy absorbed by the tree as it grew into heat. Winds eventually dissipate by warming the atmosphere, as do the waves they create on the oceans.

For environmental sustainability the net amount of energy taken in by the Planet must be zero or else the Planet will eventually get very hot or very cold. In either case we would die and the Planet become just another big rock in space like Mars and Venus. The amount of variation in the Earth's climate we can tolerate is of course limited, so the balance between incoming solar energy and the radiation lost to space is crucial to our survival.

Unfortunately the balance of "energy in" being equal to "energy out" is never strictly true over any period of time anyway. Crops absorb and hence store energy as they grow. They need to be burned, eaten or broken down to their most elemental constituent chemical parts to release that energy. All life stores energy while it is alive and only returns it after death. A major consequence of this phenomenon is that many millions of years ago vegetation, and a great deal of microscopic animal life, absorbed energy and over millions of years retained it. Coal and oil are simply fossilized trees and algae. They still contain much energy in the form of hydro carbons which is why we have used them as fuel. At the time they were growing they absorbed energy and hence contributed to the climatic conditions at that time. But these days, by mining coal and oil and using them for fuel, humankind has been adding energy to that received from the Sun, thereby heating the Planet. While the amount of heat is relatively small on a planetary scale, it is the release of methane when fossil fuels are mined and the production of carbon dioxide when they are used that is causing concern.

The Planet has been reasonably stable during its life of over four billion years because of its atmosphere. This acts as a buffer to insulate the Planet against extreme intakes or losses of heat. There are also other factors such as the extent of the white ice at the poles, which reflects heat away, and the stability in the chemical content of the atmosphere itself. Too little ice and the Earth begins to heat up, too much and it begins to cool down.

The ice ages are testament to periods when the areas of polar ice increased and by reducing energy intake thence accelerated the loss of heat and creation of more ice. In turn, the ice retreated after each ice age due to some other countering effect such as changes in the atmosphere. This latter effect is now called global warming and the scientific explanation is that the atmosphere contains gases which obstruct radiation losses but not radiation gains. They are thus called greenhouse gases because, like the glass in a greenhouse, they let in heat more readily than they let it out. The energy entering from the Sun is at a higher temperature (and thus in a higher frequency range) than that radiated out and the transmission of heat falls with frequency. When the concentrations of these gases increases the Planet gets hotter.

As it happens, carbon dioxide and methane are greenhouse gases and a normal product of human, animal and plant life throughout the Planet, so when the ice ages killed off much of such life the concentration of these gases dropped and the Planet warmed up again, melting the ice. The mechanism is quite complex because plants absorb carbon dioxide for some of the time and both it and methane may be captured to some extent by the oceans and tundra.

Nonetheless, scientists have been measuring the concentration of the greenhouse gases for many years. Their concentration has been rising and it correlates well with the increase in emissions of carbon dioxide, methane and other greenhouse gases since fossil fuels such as coal and oil began to be used on a large scale following the industrial revolution. So while burning fossil fuels may not release a damaging amount of energy they do emit greenhouse gases which increase the amount of the Sun's energy retained by the Planet. Contemporary plants and vegetation similarly emit carbon dioxide when used as a fuel. However such carbon dioxide is absorbed by the next generation of plants and is part of the hitherto stable energy balance before fossil fuels were utilised. Hence the use of so-called short-rotation crops for bio fuels.

Technological solutions

Could technology actually reduce harmful emissions? Of course it could. In an article published by Scientific American in 2009, Jacobson and Delucchi show how the energy we could harness from the sun, hydro and wind sources, is well in excess of the global need [6.20]. The problems are the lack of political will and the innate nature of capitalism. Human achievements bear witness to the things of which it is capable and as this book repeatedly emphasises it is not what technology could do but the way in which capitalism distorts the objectives and constrains technology to what it actually does.

When in the 1960s John F. Kennedy, President of the USA, called for the US to win the race to put a man on the moon to demonstrate the superiority of the US socio-economic-political system over that of Russia,

US technology placed men on the moon within eight years. But it needed political will. The President had to persuade Congress and the Senate to allocate the funds to do so. The constraints of free-market capitalism were bypassed to achieve the President's goal. From an holistic viewpoint it might also be argued that the investment in the space race by the USA was to ensure the continuation of free-market capitalism, the centre piece of the USA's system, and was therefore simply a free-market promotional exercise to be funded from longer term US profits. One doubts whether this argument was raised or put explicitly to the US voters.

Whatever the motivation, the point is that survival (in the above case that of a culture and system) was achieved by a major development programme for which no immediate financial justification was possible. The value of this programme was in its contribution to sustaining the then western culture.

We have a similar need today, to address "value" which is not expressible in the simple terms of capitalism, that of an immediate return on investment. The knowledge and technical capabilities are already available to reduce carbon emissions, to deploy more sustainable methods of energy production and to recycle waste. Chris Goodall's recent book, "Ten technologies to save the Planet" explains very succinctly what is possible [6.21]. There is no mystery about how to reduce the energy losses from buildings or migrate from oil to other fuels on which to run transport. There are many excellent books on the subject and innumerable research conferences and publications devoted to the relevant technologies. In 50 years time the first generation of such technologies may look like a model T Ford in comparison to a Formula 1 car, but there are no technical obstacles. There are also plenty of embryonic good ideas such as the use of algae and bacteria to produce oil directly and the use of high-voltage, direct-current transmission. This latter could be used to convey huge quantities of electricity to the centres of population from banks of photovoltaic panels laid out in desert sun. The two main obstacles are firstly that all these technologies currently cost more than those used hitherto to provide energy in a useable form and secondly that the value of addressing climate change is not universally perceived and accepted.

In regard to the first, and to their credit, the UK and several other European governments have devised a variety of ways in which to either subsidise investment in renewable sources of energy or penalise those which continue to use fuels which generate harmful emissions. There are broadly three methods; two "carrots" and one "stick".

1. **Feed-in Tariffs (FIT).** Owners of small renewable energy schemes may obtain a subsidy from the Government for each unit of energy they generate as well as receiving the going rate for selling that same energy. In the UK the subsidy has been calculated on the basis that for a typical renewable energy project the return for the investor would be around 6% per year thereby encouraging new investment and schemes. Such schemes apply to domestic scale installations of a kilowatt or so, such as roof-mounted, photovoltaic, solar panels and wind turbines, as well as outright commercial installations.

2. **Renewable Obligation Certificates (ROCs).** These are intended to be transnational and priced at what the market itself determines according to supply and demand. They are based on giving any producer of renewable energy a certificate (ROC) for each megawatt hour (MWh) of energy produced. The ROCs may thence be sold in the market place at the going rate. A combined heat and power system which uses biomass to produce electricity and its waste heat to supply an industrial process will get more ROCs per MWh than a diesel-generator supplying electricity alone because it makes more use of the energy residing in the fuel. The major utilities are required by Government to deliver a target number of ROCs each year, which they may create themselves through renewable energy projects or buy in the market place.

3. **Climate Change Levy.** All consumers pay a levy on the energy they use. This is collected by the utilities when they bill their customers and thence pass it on to the Government. There is thus an incentive for all consumers and especially large industrial users, to reduce their consumption of energy and hence the levy. They may also buy ROCs in the market place and since each ROC entitles them to a reduction in the levy they are in a position to make straightforward cost-benefit calculations to determine their actions and how much to invest in higher efficiency, the purchase of ROCs or the payment of the levy.

There are many alternative technologies and hence choices as to which should be given emphasis or priority. The winners and losers for one option will be different to those for another. Wind turbines may offend a proportion of the rural population while wave-power will probably upset some who live on the coast. One approach may create jobs and another stimulate imports. It is therefore not easy for a government to act even when it wishes to do so because there are many opportunities for political dissent and argument. The feed-in tariffs referred to above were only recently announced in the UK and apply to barely 2% of potential electricity generation. There is also a developing problem because the increase in small renewable energy schemes is by its very nature distributed. The existing grids and distribution networks for gas and electricity were originally developed to provide a reliable service to customers from relatively few large central power plants (maybe a hundred). These networks are a crucially important part of the UK infrastructure yet in the ownership of large transnational companies. To change the networks to facilitate the distributed connections of many thousands of small energy sources is not just costly but difficult to manage. It is impractical to quickly replace a system which has taken 100 years to establish, so who decides when and where to start? The changes also involve a revision of the methods of automatic control which is essential but technically complex and difficult to achieve piecemeal across a nationally integrated, physically interconnected system.

The UK government's decision process meanwhile grinds away exceedingly slowly. It has been driven for many of the past 25 years, regardless of political colour, by leaders whose education has suffered in the very ways described above. They appear to have been influenced more by unelected individual advisers and the lobbyists of the large corporations with a vested interest in the status quo, than an informed civil service. All are reasons why a single, systemic change which encourages sustainable actions at the transaction level of activity, is likely to be so much more effective and just. If the transactions by every citizen reflected the impact of their decisions on the lifestyle and finances of themselves, how irrelevant would the lobbyist and the politicians become in matters of the environment. This is the practical route to the *Big Society*.

Notes and references for chapter 6

6.1   Roger Scrutton, *Kant*, Oxford University Press, 1992, ISBN 0-19-287578-7.

6.2   Bryan Magee, *Popper*, Fontana, 1985, ISBN 0-00-686008-7.

6.3   *The Meaning of Life*
Just remember that you're standing on a planet that's evolving
And revolving at nine hundred miles an hour,
That's orbiting at nineteen miles a second, so it's reckoned,
A sun that is the source of all our power.
The sun and you and me and all the stars that we can see
Are moving at a million miles a day
In an outer spiral arm, at forty thousand miles an hour,
Of the galaxy we call the 'Milky Way'.
Our galaxy itself contains a hundred billion stars.
It's a hundred thousand light years side to side.
It bulges in the middle, sixteen thousand light years thick,
But out by us, it's just three thousand light years wide.
We're thirty thousand light years from galactic central point.
We go 'round every two hundred million years,
And our galaxy is only one of millions of billions
In this amazing and expanding universe.
The universe itself keeps on expanding and expanding
In all of the directions it can whizz
As fast as it can go, at the speed of light, you know,
Twelve million miles a minute, and that's the fastest speed there is.
So remember, when you're feeling very small and insecure,
How amazingly unlikely is your birth,
And pray that there's intelligent life somewhere up in space,
'Cause there's bugger all down here on Earth.
From the Monty Python film, 1983.

6.4   Al Gore, *An Inconvenient Truth: The Planetary Emergency of Global Warming and What We Can Do About it*, Bloomsbury Publishing PLC, 2006, ISBN-10: 0747589062,   ISBN-13: 978-0747589068.

6.5   Snow, C. P., *The Two Cultures*, Cambridge University Press, Canto Edition, 1993, ISBN 0 521 06520 8 (hb), ISBN 0 521 45730 0 (pb).

6.6   Niccolo Machiavelli, *The Prince,* (Translation by George Bull), Penguin Classics, 1961, ISBN 0-14-044107-7

6.7   Gabriel Kron, *Tensors for Circuits,* Dover Publications Inc.,1959.

6.8   Tracey Emin, *Mattress, linens, pillows, objects,* 1998, Saatchi Gallery - London Contemporary Art Gallery.

6.9   Damien Hirst, *Away from the Flock, 1994, composed of a dead sheep in a glass tank of formaldehyde.*

6.10   *Terminal 5 was commissioned in 2008 and on the opening day chaos ensued for which the entire enterprise was pilloried as another example of British incompetence.*
Terminal 5 cost in excess of £4.2 billion to build and is unique. The design may owe much to experience gained from other terminals at other airports but in its details it is a "one-off". More than this, its function is to expedite the activities of thousands of people and hundreds of airlines every day, each of which has a myriad of activities to which it (or they) are connected and which must be coordinated for it (or them) to carry out their own functions. Its connection with the terminal may be the start or culmination of their activities and anything in between. It is a very complicated matter with thousands of stakeholders beyond the airline and terminal operators. Thousands of component activities are going on at any one time and must simultaneously succeed, or at least be under control, to avoid chaos.
To get a feel for how complexity and failures are related, consider a motor car made from say 5000 components. For illustration purposes, assume that each and every component has a 0.001 chance of failing (i.e. 1 in a 1000) and hence disabling the entire car. The chances of the car being in working condition is (0.999) to the power 5000 which is such a small number that any car built from such components is almost certain to fail. Which is why it has taken nearly 100 years to reach the standards of car reliability we enjoy today. In practice the components in a car are expected to have failure rates of typically 1 in a million or better.
Terminal 5 at Heathrow is and always has been a magnificent achievement as an engineering construction and as an example of how to deliver to time

and budget. Its accident rate during construction was below the average for the industry. No engineer would have commissioned it in its totality in one day because the numbers of things which might go wrong were enormous, especially the human elements and the bespoke baggage handling systems. Any one thing may have had a small probability of failure and what might go wrong was unpredictable. But that something would go wrong is totally predictable and across all potential failures a certainty. The attempt to implement the new terminal by BA in one day was therefore idiotic and the ensuing chaos totally foreseeable. It was of course commissioned in that way by executives from a company without any engineering or scientific expertise.

6.11   *In 2008 the UK Government removed the lowest rate of income tax of 10p in favour of a flat rate of 20%. The net effect was to partly fund a reduction in tax on the better off from an increase in tax on a large segment of the poor. This was eventually corrected after a major political row and considerable public outcry. Amazingly, the initial, televised response from the Chief Secretary to the Treasury, was that the original change was alright "because the number of individuals who benefit from the tax changes outnumber those who do not".*

And in 2008 the UK rate of VAT was cut from 17.5% to 15%. This coincided with a change of tax on wine from £1.46 to £1.57 a bottle. The net effect is a rise in price for lower-price wines below £5.95 per bottle and a reduction for all wines costing more than that. Again a boost for the well off who can afford expensive wine and a penalty for the poor who cannot.

I feel sure the Government did not really intend to penalise the poor in either case. It and the civil service are simply not numerate. They do not adequately check the effect of their decisions nor do they appear to be alert to the possibility of arithmetical aberrations when formulating policy.

In September 2010, Her Majesty's Revenue and Customs 2009-10 report and accounts reveal that it has been unable to deal with the bulk of a backlog of 18.2m unreconciled cases dating back to the 2004-05 tax year. The report says many of those affected "may not be aware that they have overpaid tax and are due a refund or, where they have underpaid, that they are liable to make further payments". It went on: "The amounts involved are substantial, which early analysis suggests could in aggregate lead to tax repayments and recoveries of £3bn and £1.4bn respectively". Around 4.3 million have paid too much and are due a refund, worth £1.8bn, while 1.4 million have underpaid a total £2bn and will have to pay an average of £1,428 each in further tax.

The report also states that the backlog of open cases could take a further four years to clear.

6.12 *"Science is too important not to be a part of popular culture. To explore the universe is a noble goal, and one we have a responsibility to pursue vigorously. After all, it has taken 13.7 billion years for hydrogen atoms to arrange themselves into these patterns we call human beings that can build machines to gaze deep into the heart of matter and marvel at the beauty of it all.*
It would be a shame if the ultimate result of billions of years of nuclear alchemy in the heart of billions and billions of suns were considered by the majority to be a pattern of atoms called Simon Cowell."
Professor Brian Cox, University of Manchester, referring to the Large Hadron Collider which was switched on at CERN, Switzerland in September, 2008.

6.13 Tony Blair, *A Journey,* Hutchinson, 2010, ISBN 10: 009192555X, ISBN 13: 978-0091925550.

6.14 James Gleick, *Chaos: Making a New Science,* Penguin, 1988, ISBN-10: 0140092501, ISBN-13: 978-0140092509.

6.15 Davies, P.C.W. and Brown, J., *Superstrings: A Theory of Everything,* Cambridge University Press, Canto Edition, 1988, ISBN 0 521 43775 X.

6.16 Peter Coveney and Roger Highfield, *Frontiers of Complexity: The Search for Order in a Chaotic World,* Faber and Faber,1995, ISBN 0-571 -16691-0.

6.17 *Neal Zining is responsible for the particular calculation and presentation of the images reproduced in Figure 6.3. see also http://users.erols. com/ziring/mandel.html*

6.18 Fritjof Capra, *The Web of Life: A New Synthesis of Mind and Matter,* Harper Collins, 1996, ISBN 0 00 255499 2.

6.19   Michael Gibbons, Camille Limoges, Helga Nowotny, Simon Schwartzman, Peter Scott and Martin Trow, *The new production of knowledge,* Sage, 1995, ISBN 0-8039-7794-8.

6.20   *Wind, water and solar technologies can provide 100 percent of the world's energy, eliminating all fossil fuels. Supplies of wind and solar energy on accessible land dwarf the energy consumed by people around the globe.*

- *The authors' plan calls for 3.8 million large wind turbines, 90,000 solar plants, and numerous geothermal, tidal and rooftop photovoltaic installations worldwide.*
- *The cost of generating and transmitting power would be less than the projected cost per kilowatt-hour for fossil-fuel and nuclear power.*
- *Shortages of a few specialty materials, along with lack of political will, loom as the greatest obstacles.*

Mark Z. Jacobson, and Mark A. Delucchi, Scientific American Magazine, November, 2009.

6.21   Chris Goodall, *Ten technologies to save the Planet,* Green Profile, 2008, ISBN 978 1 84668 868 3

Chapter 7:
The *Big Society*

"Happiness is not an ideal of reason but of imagination."

Emmanuel Kant (1724-1804)

For reasons of sustainability, requisite variety, bounded rationality and the avoidance of chaos, a systemic change to capitalism is essential. The simple and easily comprehended idea of involving the Planet as a stakeholder in the capitalist system would seem to provide the mechanism for achieving such change. This is also a practical basis for the *Big Society*.

Concept

As it currently operates, capitalism is driven by self-interest and requires growth. But, unless growth can be achieved without net consumption the human race will be unable to sustain itself over the long term because the Planet's biosphere is fragile and its resources finite. This would be true even without the probability of human-induced climate change. It would be true regardless of the need to prevent the repeated, banker-led financial crises which punish millions of innocent taxpayers while continuing to reward those same bankers on an obscenely large scale.

Unfortunately the development of capitalism has forged a niche which takes no account of the fragility of the Planet to our presence nor of the finite limit to its resources. We and the myriad of traditions and institutions which characterise the human condition have evolved and continue to evolve to suit this niche without questioning the assumptions which underpin it. The Planet is not benign nor infinitely resourceful. Our human-forged niche conveys the message that we survive if we have money and die if we don't. Monetary wealth equates to success and poverty to failure. Governments are increasingly followers of what capitalism desires rather than its masters. Even a cursory examination of capitalism indicates that it does not have sufficient flexibility and variety of response that a rapidly changing environment requires (Ashby's requisite variety, Chapter 2).

Scientists agree that sustainability is practical and that we can adapt to climate change. Engineers already have the means by which adaption and mitigation can be achieved. Technology can thus deliver a solution (Chapter 6). But both leadership and politics, so essential to drive change are transient and top-down. They need to be supplemented with practical methods of motivating and implementing change bottom-up; the goal of the *Big Society*. Moreover, because the capitalist system is practically universal, a systemic change is required if the human species is to survive.

In regard to capitalism itself, the most recent financial crisis of 2008 has left the people angered just as they were in the previous crises, particularly those of 1908 and 1929. But, unlike previous crises for which all the promises of it never being allowed to happen again were broken, things have changed. The global population, the UK, Europe, Japan and USA in particular, are more fully educated, more worldly and less deferential to their political leaders, industrial and financial bosses.

So, paradoxically, the global financial crisis of 2008 may turn out to be a helpful factor in stimulating change. It is clear that the lessons of the 1908 and 1933 crises were poorly learned and regulatory action to remedy the problem has been demonstrably inadequate. For the moment then, we have both a financial-system imperative and a climate-change imperative to drive change. We also have an ongoing and urgent need to reduce global poverty.

There is thus a unique opportunity to do something systemic, more substantial and globally more effective than mere regulation, which self-evidently changes with the direction of the political wind and is inadequate. We need something which better aligns the pursuit of self-interest, that inherent property of humankind which is both a curse and a salvation, with the self-interest of the Planet; something which might also provide a more equitable and less volatile distribution of wealth. If we don't do this the Planet will surely win on terms we will regret.

Why could governments not simply decree the necessary steps? Well the book has gone to some lengths to demonstrate that the human condition is so complex that no one can understand it in its totality (Simon's bounded rationality, Chapter 4). Top-down policy initiatives can therefore be dangerous and lead to unintended consequences. The real world consists of many interconnections (see complexity, Chapter 5) and they mostly combine to form what technologists describe as "non-linear systems". We now understand the chaos that can be caused by small local changes to such systems (Lorenz, Chapter 6). It is also highly improbable that the 200+ countries of the globe, each with regular changes of government, could agree to align their separate policies (assuming even that such policies would be "right") with an appropriate global policy and maintain it indefinitely - a point borne out by the historical failure to avoid financial crises and deal with rogue states and poverty.

The failure by Greece to abide by its obligations to keep its national finances within the boundaries set by the European Union, even as a condition of joining the Union, is at the time of writing, in danger of wrecking the euro as a credible currency. The G20 conference of finance ministers in Beijing in 2010 failed to get the Chinese to agree to revalue its currency to protect western economies. The problem for the western economies is their perceived need to grow themselves out of their recessions while cutting back on government spending. But someone and some countries have to buy the exported goods to enable this to happen. If they are all compromised in this way there is no way out of the mess unless those unaffected by the problem buy those exports. But why should they? Something more effective than negotiation is required.

More fundamentally still, governments can only deal with the human condition as they find and perceive it. If the human condition had evolved in a different kind of niche (i.e. something other than free-market capitalism) it would almost certainly have created different institutions and traditions to those we currently have. Setting top-down policies for institutions and traditions which are a product of surviving in the existing niche is merely to err from the outset. Top-down policies are bound to fail because all the relationships and statistics relate to the current structures which are to varying degrees inappropriate.

However, if we change our niche by systemic intervention we will get a steady movement (i.e. evolution), from what we have to something else. The important thing is to ensure the intervention affects the basic transactions and processes in the desired way. It is more practical and scientifically correct to intervene systemically. How exactly the aggregated outcomes turn out and our institutions and traditions change thereafter is unclear; an evolutionary process albeit with losers as well as winners. But if the most elemental transactions of humankind are constrained to those which serve the interests of both humankind and the planet then the aggregated result should be in those interests too.

The concept is of applying a single, simple idea universally – just one pill for the globe's nations to swallow. The idea is that a sustainable future is more likely if every individual is caused to explicitly include the value of the Planet in every one of his or her value transactions. The suggestion is to include the Planet as a stakeholder alongside all other stakeholders in the global, capitalist system. It may currently be perceived as a free market but unless the Planet is included, that market is fundamentally incomplete. We are fooling ourselves, we are stealing from the Planet.

This is not advocating a top-down approach in the conventional sense of a government setting politically fomented policies. Governments and leaders are not, under this proposition, expected to tell people what to do from their helicopter yet incomplete and bounded view of the world. It is simply proposing that they all accept the universal point that if we are to continue sustainably on this planet then all activity must be sustainable. How individuals and organisations at the elemental level choose to collaborate and develop to ensure that those unsustainable activities are offset by sustainable ones is a matter for them. The role of government, through the law, financial systems and leaders, is to ensure compliance. Net outcomes will then be sustainable. The structures and methods by which sustainability is achieved will be evolutionary, a bottom-up affair which will develop naturally. Along the way it will no doubt be subject to a variety of political winds but the fundamental solution will be in place out of political control per se.

Mechanism

The mechanism is to represent the Planet as an owner of wealth in the current capitalist system, an alter ego for the Planet which trades with and alongside everyone else. If, as is demonstrated in practice, we can globally accept the idea and disciplines of an International Monetary Fund (IMF), we ought to be able to accept the idea and disciplines of a Planet Conservation Fund (PCF); my term for this surrogate for the Planet. This is the key assumption, much depending on the "ought" rather than the more wishful "should" but it builds on a successful precedent (IMF) and is a singular and simple requirement. The PCF might even be an integral part of the IMF. The proposition that a change to the capitalist system is a necessary step in the interest of us all offers **a** better prospect than major unrest and a confrontation with capitalism akin to that of the 1917 revolution in Russia only more widespread. The proposition is that:

"The Planet should charge through the PCF for things which deplete it and pay for things which regenerate it."

Given that this proposition were to be accepted, there are many detailed ways of implementing it. The following is JUST ONE idea.

The charges may be regarded as a kind of tax but they differ conceptually from conventional taxes because they are not for the benefit of any government per se. The Planet's taxes can be positive or negative and the net value should ultimately fall to zero once an environmentally sustainable future has been achieved. Depletion and regeneration would then be equal. It is only during the initial period that the net tax would be positive (i.e. payments to the Planet). However, the initial surplus is itself a benefit because it could invested on behalf of the Planet in environmentally sustainable projects, and distributed to those countries which are either low consumers of, or net regenerators of, the Planet's resources. The Planet would not make a profit at any stage. The tax would be a stick to discourage unsustainable practices and an incentive to encourage sustainable ones.

To facilitate acceptance of the approach, the initial taxes levied on the Planet's behalf would be very low and relatively simple, even crude. They would then rise in a pre-announced way and in more detail based on ever-improving data, to increase the pressure for change. As change became evident and effective the net tax would fall.

The world has nearly seven billion stakeholders who variously engage with the monetary system. To add the Planet makes it about seven billion and one. Yet the result is a mechanism with three powerful attributes and a major consequence:

Attribute 1: Firstly, it aligns the capitalist system more effectively with Ashby's Law of requisite variety by increasing its scope to respond to changes that threaten us and matter to us. Humankind is not actually living within a human-forged niche – stay in credit or be damned. We are living on a Planet in which not just money but multiple criteria determine whether we are damned or not – temperature, pollution, water, food, shelter, resources, plant and animal diversity, poverty and excessive population. Our systems of self-control, aspiration and government must therefore extend these features which are literally "taken into account" in our system of valuing things.

Attribute 2: Secondly, it continues to allow the pursuit of self interest. For long periods the free market has operated well because it is notionally self-regulating and individuals at the base of the economic pyramid through to those at the top, all use the same self-interest criterion of monetary value when they buy, sell, invest or save. But free-market capitalism is failing because of greed (unregulated pursuit of self interest) , the excessive power of large corporations (which can squash competition) and the ability of financial institutions to obtain vast quantities of money from the use of money itself (no tangible exchange of value). It is also inadequate in its coverage of what is truly of value, not because it doesn't broadly work.

Any payment for products or services with the Planet as a stakeholder, would contain a charge, an element of cost, whenever those services and products have involved use of the Planet's resource. The charge would be the cumulative and net result of the transactions which involved the Planet's resources in creating the product or service. Some charges would be positive and some negative. The latter representing transactions which restore, rather than destroy, the Planet's resources, such as the recovery of materials from waste and the absorbing of carbon dioxide from fossil-fuel-driven emissions.

Two new categories of money would be needed to implement in this method of involving the Planet. Accountants already distinguish capital- and revenue-type transactions by simply defining them as such even though each is measured in sums of the single parameter money (be it in pounds, dollars, Euros, yen or whatever). So, with the new categories of money, it should be possible to keep track of how much of a given transaction is to be apportioned to the Planet.

So if I purchase a motor car it is feasible for me to pay £X for the car and receive not just the car but also some (new) money accompanying that car, which specifies how much of the car's price represents resources owned by the Planet. That is $X = P + Y$, where P is the Planet's share and Y the amount for the labour and material content of the car itself. X, P and Y are distinguished separately in the accounts of both the seller and myself. The amount P is effectively the Planet's share and would be distinguished by consisting of similar style and value notes as those used for X and Y but say red rather than blue, the colour of ordinary currency, and clearly designated as the Planet's.

Actually there would need to be two types of Planet note not just red because the Planet would sometimes be paid for the depletion of resources and sometimes need to pay back for the regeneration of its resources. The quantity P in the above example would always be positive in the equation $X = P + Y$ but since the quantity P may represent depletion in some cases and regeneration in others the two cases must be distinguished. For explanation purposes let us say red for depletion and green for regeneration.

If electronic accounting were used rather than coloured cash, the red and green would simply be identified under separate headings in those accounts. Information technology is almost ubiquitous and hence a major facilitator for this purpose; a further reason why now is an opportune time for introducing change.

The operational requirement is innovative. It requires that any exchange for money of goods or services should be accompanied by an exchange indicating the content owed or owing to the Planet by monetary value. Whoever buys the goods or service automatically takes on the credit or debt to the Planet as represented in the Planet's share. So, at any one time any individual and organization would have an account with three kinds of currency – 1. Normal (blue), 2. Planet credit (green), and 3. Planet debt (red). As an ongoing process, any individuals or organisations would be able to settle their accounts in part or whole with the PCT through a bank or whatever PCT-determined agency. They would hand in their Planet currencies and depending on whether the net value was a credit or debit, receive or pay the PCT in normal currency to that value. For its part, the PCT would then re-issue the credits and debits to those using or renewing the Planet's resources, adjusting over time, the charges and payments for each resource according to the type of resource.

The further opportunity to reduce poverty lies in the ability of the PCT to issue credits to poverty-stricken inhabitants of the third-world who use less than average of the Planet's resources and create considerably fewer harmful emissions. Since the credits could be turned directly into cash, the mechanism is linked to the Planet's mainstream economic system and opens up new possibilities to reduce poverty.

Examples:

A mining company

The mine depletes the Planet and would be liable for charges from the Planet (PCF) and receive from the PCF red notes at the going rate per unit of its output (for example £p per tonne). This would appear in the company's accounts as a debt to the Planet (PCF). However, as the output were sold each item could pass on some of the charges to the customers in the form of red notes and so reduce the amount owed to the Planet by the company. Shareholders in the company would be expected to pay some of the charges as a proportion of outstanding debt to the Planet. Dividends and share issues would similarly include both normal and planetary (red note) currencies. The actual proportions would be based on the usual social, economic and political calculations and national policies although the base charges would be defined globally by the PCF.

A manufacturing company such as a car assembly plant

The company purchases components which contain raw materials mined or recycled or from the sun. At every stage in the supply chain each transaction to buy in goods or services would exchange money for those services and receive, in addition to each, a quantity of the Planet's currency, as in $X=P+Y$ above. The amount of Planet's currency would depend of course on the charges set by the PCF. When the company issues shares or dividends to shareholders or sells a car it would pass some of the Planet's currency on with the dividend, deducting or adding the debit or credit respectively from the dividend itself. It would not pass any Planet's currency to its employees because they have not received any Planet's resource nor do they own any of the company's resources or value.

Although the magnitude of charges would be set by the PCF, the distribution of charges for the Planet's resources across those who use them, is a matter of regulation and ultimately a local political choice, as are the charges for those who renew the Planet's resources; examples of the increased degrees of freedom with which to manage complexity (Ashby's Law).

Over a reasonable period of time such as a year or two (another political choice), any organisation such as this company, would need to ensure that the net value of P falls to zero. To achieve this it could try to obtain its components and energy from suppliers which have a zero or negative charge from the Planet. Or at least attempt to ensure that across all suppliers the net value of P, that is the sum of positive and negative Planet currencies, is low. The mechanism thereby puts pressure on organisations to become sustainable.

A *wind-farm company*

As for the mining company above, the initial purchases of wind turbines and associated plant will incur charges as the suppliers pass on part of the debt or credit to the Planet incurred when they buy in goods derived from mined products. This debt or credit (most likely debt at this initial stage) must therefore be reflected in charges to customers and shareholders. However, the main output from the wind farm will be electricity derived from wind which is a result of incoming solar radiation. Such radiation does not deplete the Planet and no charges by, or on, the Planet would be necessary. The amount of debt to the Planet is likely to be small in relation to the credit value of total output and would lead to net income from the PCF once the initial debts to the Planet of the turbines and installation had been offset.

Hydro-electric, tidal, wave and photovoltaic electricity generating companies would operate in a similar way to the wind-farm company.

A *waste disposal company*

There are several types of such companies but they would each operate broadly as follows depending on the mix of waste and how they dispose of it. As an example of the proposed mechanism working they are generic. This is because some of their inputs will have debts to the PCF and some not. Some of the outputs such as phosphorous and other recovered metals which renew the Planet's resources would earn significant credits.

Thus a waste disposal company which generates electricity from burning waste food will be able to claim regeneration credits from the PCF, for example *if the ash contains potash and may be used as a fertilizer, and thence pass them onto customers.*

As an electricity supplier to the above car company, it would enable the car company to receive credits and be able to offer some of them with its products or simply offset PCF debts.

However food is partly but not wholly a depleting resource and will carry with it, even in waste form, some debits. In the bigger picture the relative value of the PCF debits and credits should ensure that utilising waste in this way is beneficial. However, because the chemistry of crops, photosynthesis, combustion and the carbon dioxide cycle is complex, the calculations are complex.

A waste company which merely buries waste will simply accumulate the debts and credits in its inputs. One which recovers materials and processes them to a form which is re-useable would be able to claim credits from the PCF and pass them onto customers and shareholders.

All employed individuals

All employees would be paid in traditional currency for the reason given in the above example and would not pick up PCF debts or credits whatever these might be for their employing company. However should they purchase items of any kind in their private and domestic lives, they would have to pay the appropriate Planet's costs as in $X=P+Y$ above. It is likely that most will initially incur charges to the Planet but will gradually find increasing opportunities to buy items with a regeneration element and have a cash incentive to seek them out. This brings sustainability directly into the free-market mechanism, driven by self interest.

Banks

In the early days of implementation the values placed on P by the PCF must be small on debits (and possibly large on credits), increasing only slowly as the market develops and experience accumulates. The role of the banks is five-fold.

   a)   *To act as local agents for the PCF and manage its savings and invest-ment funds in line with best international practices, PCF policies and regulations*

b)   *To provide the means for individuals and companies to cancel equal quantities of their credits and debits with the Planet and hence return them to the PCF*

c)   *To provide an opportunity for those with a surfeit of debits with the Planet to return them to the Planet (PCF) by paying a fee and for those in credit to receive payments. These payments would be in traditional currency, at a rate determined by the PCF*

d)   *To support mechanisms whereby debits or credits are initially issued to those companies which initiate depletion or renewal of the Planet's resources*

e)   *To support mechanisms for redistributing PCF profits to promote regeneration and reduce poverty*

Investors

Investors would have to take a share of the debts or credits due to the PCF in both the initial take up of shares and subsequent dividends. Such items as "value per share" and "dividend per share" would each have a value in traditional currency and one indicating net credit or indebtedness to the Planet.. This would stimulate more investment in sustainable businesses and the enormous returns to investment banks would be moderated in future by the need to balance the PCF accounts as well as the normal ones

Poverty stricken citizens in the third world

The third world does not deplete the Planet in the same way or on the same scale as the industrialised world so its debt to the Planet would be small. Citizens in the third world would be candidates for receiving support from the PCF. They are often well-placed to produce energy from solar sources for which they would incur no charges from the PCF because the energy is renewable and not from the Planet per se (sun's input is external). Large scale photovoltaic plant exporting electricity from the sunny regions of Africa would be free from PCF charges once the initial costs of the panels had been paid off, and thus potentially a highly competitive form of energy.

The more difficult requirement is setting monetary value on resources taken from the Planet and assigning values to those returned; this is clearly a matter to be settled by the PCF. But as explained above, the initial values would be small, even zero in some cases, and only with experience and over time would they be raised.

Attribute 3: Thirdly, it acknowledges that for reasons of bounded rationality, the increasingly complex human condition and potential for chaos, that top-down political "management" is inadequate. The mechanism is an adjustment to the existing capitalist system, applicable at the grass-roots' level and capable of aggregation at all levels above. It is an attribute which strengthens the concept of the *Big Society* and delivers a mechanism to support it.

Outcomes

There are of course the likely consequences of such a change. The proposed mechanism introduces the value of the Planet and hence the Planet's self interest in the global, free-market economy. The Planet's self interest will thereby influence all human behaviour and bear on the selective development or decline of many aspects of its social, environmental, economic and even political structures. Given the above point about all our individual and corporate accounts having a record of how much we owe to the use of the Planet's resources at any one time, there will be incentives to minimise the total by trading in goods and services which have a regeneration or totally self-sustaining element in them. The ideal is for everyone, or collaborating groups in practice, to achieve a zero net balance for all "P" because that means sustainability has been achieved. At some stage it would become uneconomic for the oil companies to flare and waste huge quantities of gas in Nigeria [1.33] and for waste to become valued as a source of recycled materials, something to re-sell back to the Planet.

But, just as the systemic effect of current free-market capitalism has led to unpredictable developments in the evolution of humankind and the aforementioned structures, so will the modified system. It is impractical for politicians (or anyone else) to predict what the future will be for the human race once the interests of the Planet are fully represented in day-to-day transactions. An obvious consequence will be that the subject of economics will need to adjust. The Planet is self-evidently richer than the richest person or state and the idea that somehow politicians will be able to successfully confront climate change and achieve a sustainable future for humankind by top-down decisions and policies within the existing system of capitalism is ludicrous.

All they (we) can do is ensure that the Planet's interests are an integral consideration in everyone's daily life whenever a free-market transaction is made. **The detail is then within the grasp of the *Big Society* which must somehow free us from the human-created niche we call capitalism which favours the survival of the rich at the expense of the Planet and the poor.** What global structures will gradually emerge are anyone's guess but they are likely to be different to what we have now. The structure and traditions of a civilisation which is sustainable will not be the same as those of our current civilisation. Changing a few power stations and offering bio-fuel at the petrol pumps will not be enough. This is not because I think so but because of what Darwin, Ashby, Simon, Koestler and Malthus have said and can teach us.

Index